A Piece of the Mountain

The Story of Blaise Pascal

by Joyce McPherson

Illustrated by Jennifer B. Robinson

Dedicated to my grandmother, Marie Wydo.

© Copyright 1995, Greenleaf Books, LLC

All rights reserved. No part of this work may be
reproduced or used in any form by any means — graphic,
electronic, or mechanical including photocopying,
recording, taping or information storage and retrieval
systems without written permission from the publisher.
Internet: www.greenleafpress.com

www.greenleafpress.com
1570 Old Laguardo Rd
Lebanon, TN 37087

Table of Contents

Chapter 1

Moving Day

In the empty room a young boy gazed intently at the pattern of sunshine on the bare floor boards. He wanted to remember every detail of this room where he had spent so many happy days. Already dust had settled in the place of furniture. The boy traced his name in the dust: Blaise Pascal. He liked to practice writing it in the fancy script which his father had taught him. It made him feel older than his seven years.

The sound of other footsteps startled him. They sounded louder now that all the tapestries and furniture were gone. Blaise stopped and listened to the footsteps carefully. Yes, they were louder. Why would that be?

His thoughts were interrupted by a familiar voice. "Blaise, where are you?" It was his five-year-old sister, Jaqueline.

"I'm here!" he yelled back, enjoying the new way his voice sounded in the empty rooms.

Jaqueline's footsteps made a skipping sound up the stairs, then she burst into the room. "Papa has been looking for you everywhere!" she exclaimed. She pretended to scold Blaise, but he knew she was enjoying the flurry and excitement of their last minute preparations.

Blaise stole a last glance at the huge window that filled the room with light. Even with Papa's desk gone, this room was his favorite.

"Blaise! Are you listening?" Jaqueline tugged at his hands and jumped up and down in front of him. "If you don't come now, Papa will send Gilberte and we will both be in trouble."

"I'm coming," Blaise answered her. He lingered one last moment before he followed her down the stairs. Silently they passed through the first floor which Papa rented out as shops. Jaqueline led him into the tiny courtyard that connected the two parts of the Pascal home. Blaise thought of how they enjoyed playing "Hotel des Vernines" here. They would pretend they lived a hundred years ago when the courtyard was surrounded by a glamorous five-storied building and the row of shops were the stables.

Jaqueline must have been thinking the same thing. She held out her dress as though she were dancing at a ball and twirled her way across the courtyard. Blaise would have joined the game, but he noticed his older sister, Gilberte, in the doorway opposite to them.

"What are you two doing?" asked Gilberte. She stood with her arms folded and her back straight. She seemed older than her eleven years.

Jaqueline made a deep bow and said in her most grown-up voice, "Oh, your majesty, I would be delighted to dance with you."

"Really, playing the "Hotel des Vernines" at a time like this," replied Gilberte. She held out her hand to Jaqueline. "Come on, the coach is ready." Her words brought Blaise back to the reality of France in 1631. He met her gaze and nodded that he understood. Quietly the three children walked through the second part of the house and out the door that opened onto a narrow, sloping street.

They found their father already in the coach. Like Blaise, he seemed to be thinking of something else. He brightened when he saw his three children. "There you are. I was wondering if I would have to leave without you!"

"Papa, you would not do that, would you?" Jaqueline asked him.

"No, my little Jaquette, I could never leave you," he answered tenderly.

Jaqueline crawled onto his lap. "I'm ready to go now."

Gilberte and Blaise climbed into the coach, too. Then with creaking wheels, the heavily-laden coach began its careful descent down the narrow street.

"Blaise, wait!" A boy dashed from one of the doorways and ran alongside the coach. It was Florin Périer, Blaise's best friend. He held a chunk of something black in his outstretched hand.

Blaise leaned as far out the window of the coach as he could. For a moment their hands met as the black something passed from one boy to the other.

Breathlessly Florin explained, "Volcanic rock...from

the Puy de Dome...So you won't forget us." He stopped at the side of the road and waved to his friend.

Blaise waved the black stone and shouted, "Papa says we will see you next summer!"

Florin grinned and yelled, "Next summer."

Blaise ducked back into the coach and waved until the coach turned a corner, and he could no longer see his friend. Then he settled back in his seat to watch the town. Blaise could still see among the tangle of shorter buildings, the square outline of the cathedral which stood next to his home. As it grew smaller and smaller, he turned his attention to the small shops that lined the street. He wondered if the heavy, half-closed shutters let in much light. The road was muddy from the recent rains, and once the coach appeared to be stuck, but with careful maneuvering, the coachman coaxed it out of the rut. At the fringe of town were the houses of the poor. Blaise saw children peering from the sagging doorways of their tiny shacks. Soon after, the coach reached the gate of Clermont and glided easily through the gate of the wall that surrounded the city.

On the occasional trips that Blaise had taken through the town, this was his favorite part. Once outside the city gates, he could see vegetable gardens surrounding the wall.

"Those gardens are being grown in the moat of what used to be a walled city," his father told him.

Blaise imagined what it must have been like to live in a city that needed thick walls and a moat to ward off enemies. He looked up at the mountain, the Puy de Dome, which towered above the city of Clermont like a giant watchman. He clutched the hard, black stone in his hand, and thought to himself, "Now I have a piece of

Florin runs to give Blaise "a piece of the mountain" as the coach pulls away toward Clemont.

the mountain."

The narrow road became a wider one that took the coach and its passengers through a deep valley. Blaise stopped his daydreaming and began listening to the things Papa was saying.

Papa pointed through the window. "Do you see this valley? This is where my family came from. They were hard-workers, and over time they became more and more prosperous. My father was the Treasurer at Riom. He was also a rather independent thinker, which got him in trouble sometimes." Papa chuckled. "I guess there's a streak of stubbornness in the Pascal line." Papa's face became serious again. "After the next hill is the town where your Mother's family came from."

"Tell us about Mother, please," Jaqueline quickly interjected. Blaise leaned forward in interest. He could barely remember his mother. He was three years old when she died.

Papa was quiet for a moment. "She was a beautiful and pious woman," he said.

"Where is she now?" asked Jaqueline. She always had the same question.

Gilberte answered her. "Jaquette, you know she's in heaven!"

Her answer made Blaise think of a question. "But how do you know?"

"That is a good question," answered Papa. "There are some things you know by seeing and others that you know by believing."

Blaise watched the rolling countryside and thought about his father's answer. When the coach arrived in Paris, he was still thinking.

Chapter 2

Sound Learning

Blaise awoke to the smell of freshly baked bread from a nearby bakery. In the four years since his family had moved to Paris, he had learned to recognize the unique smell of each of the little shops near his home. He stretched and started to get out of bed, but then lay down on his pillow.

At eleven years of age he was growing quickly and often felt tired. He closed his eyes and listened to the swish of the street cleaner's broom. He could imagine the streets just beginning to fill with men and women on their way to work. There might be street sellers with baskets of fruits and vegetables on their heads. Or perhaps there would be a "seller of useful trinkets". They carried wide boxes by a strap around the neck. The boxes were full of tantalizing objects. Last week Papa let Blaise buy a thing called a fork that the vendor claimed was a new tool for eating. Blaise kept it in a special box along with the black rock from Florin. He knew Florin would want to see his find.

Blaise's reverie was interrupted by the entrance of a small, brown-haired woman. "Good morning, Blaise," she said crisply. "Your father will be waiting to talk with you at breakfast, so you had better get dressed now."

Blaise sprang out of bed and started dressing immediately. Not only did he enjoy his morning talks with his father more than anything else, he knew that Madame Delfaut was not one to tolerate lying in bed. She seemed to radiate efficiency. Everywhere she went comforters were twitched into place, dust particles disappeared off of tables, and piles of books became orderly. She had been entrusted with the care of the three Pascal children, and she took her job very seriously. "You can be sure that I always have my eye on you," she often told them. Blaise believed it!

Blaise did his best to tuck in his shirt and comb his hair to Madame Delfaut's satisfaction.

"That will do." She nodded approvingly. "Your father will be at the table by now."

Blaise scooped up some books that lay next to his bed and ran to find his father.

Every morning Blaise's father spent time with his children's lessons. But what lessons! They were different from the meaningless repetitions of facts found in the schoolbooks. Blaise's father wanted to teach his children to think. His own experience had taught him that schools often attempted to fill a pupil's heads full of facts instead of allowing the pupil to find the truth for himself. Thus,

Blaise's father had decided to leave his successful job in Clermont and devote himself to science and the instruction of his children. Learning was always interesting with Papa, and this morning was no exception.

Gilberte and Blaise had barely begun discussing their grammar lesson, when Blaise's attention was caught by something else. Jaqueline struck a porcelain plate with a knife. When Blaise touched the plate with his hand, the noise abruptly stopped.

Blaise looked at his father. "Did you hear that, Papa? The sound stopped when I touched the plate."

"Is that all you noticed?" his father asked.

Blaise struck his own plate and touched it again. "No, there's more than the sound. I can actually feel the plate wiggling."

His father smiled. "That wiggling you feel is called vibrating. It's important to use the correct words. Now, tell me what caused the vibration."

"I struck the plate with a knife," Blaise responded.

"Correct. When you struck the plate, what do you think happened?"

Blaise thought for a moment. "When I strike things hard, they either break or move. I struck the plate softly. Perhaps that caused the plate to move just a little, but then it kept on wiggling—I mean vibrating."

Papa was smiling. He leaned forward to press his point. "How could you determine if the plate was vibrating?"

"You could feel it with your hand..." Blaise stopped to think further. "The sound began when I struck the plate and began the vibrations. It ended when my hand stopped the vibrations. Does that mean that sound is vibration?" With growing excitement Blaise struck a glass with the knife. It made a clear ringing sound. He touched it with his fingers and the ringing stopped.

His father interrupted his noise-making with the raise of his hand. "As of yet, you still have only an idea that vibration is sound. You must think how you can show this is true. Are there other observations of a similar nature that you can make?"

Blaise laid aside his grammar books. Throughout the morning he could be heard tapping and banging things all over the house. From time to time he reported to his father to discuss what he had found. His father had studied the science of musical sounds and was able to guide Blaise in his experiments.

For the next few weeks Blaise used his spare time to investigate his queries about sound. His father challenged him to develop his ideas and carefully work through a method of testing them. He required Blaise to record and evaluate each step. The experimental process intrigued young Blaise. It opened up new ways of looking at the world. With the enthusiasm of a sportsman, he pursued his game. He reveled in each victory that won him another piece of information for his quest.

One particular afternoon a whoop of triumph was heard from the direction of Blaise's room. In a moment he dashed into the front room where Gilberte was sewing. Blaise's outbursts were common, and Gilberte did not even pause when she heard his shout. When she saw the jubilant expression on Blaise's face, however, she put down her sewing. "Blaise, what happened?" she asked.

Blaise perched on the footstool next to his sister and began to explain how his latest trial with vibration had worked. His words spilled over each other in his eagerness to tell her everything he had found.

Gilberte interrupted him, "Do you mean to tell me you are still working on that experiment with sound? You started it weeks ago!"

Blaise brushed aside her question and continued talking. He only paused when he had given the full explanation.

Gilberte shook her head in mock concern. "If you attack all your experiments this way, I don't know what will become of you."

Blaise did not stay to speculate. As he left the room he could not resist knocking on the heavy door frame and listening to the nice thud it made.

Chapter 3

Secret Studies

Jaqueline and Blaise sat at the dining room table which was covered with books and papers. Jaqueline was ten, and she was studying grammar. At twelve, Blaise was studying Greek and Latin. It was a cold March morning in 1636. Madame Delfaut, being a thrifty soul, kept the house barely warm enough for comfort. She insisted that the cool temperature was good for stirring up "the system."

"I wish Madame would make it warmer in the house," Jaqueline complained.

"Papa says it makes him think better," Blaise offered.

"Think? Think?" Jaqueline stood on her chair to increase the dramatic effect. "Who can think when one must study grammar?"

"Papa says we have to understand languages before we can start the other subjects. Listen to this quote from Cicero: `Nothing is more shameful then to affirm before knowing.' In Latin that's `Nihil turpius...'"

Jaqueline interrupted, "`To conquer without risk is to triumph without glory.' That is what I call language! Corneille wrote that in `El Cid', and he's still alive, unlike Cicero!"

Blaise looked suspiciously at the books and papers in front of Jaqueline. "Jaquette, what is hiding under your grammar?"

Jaqueline slid guiltily off her chair. "It's `El Cid', but I'm not reading it right now."

Blaise put down his book. He realized that he was not going to be able to study while Jaqueline was in this mood. "May I ask what you are doing, then?"

Jaqueline pretended to ignore him while she delicately placed each of her papers into a neat pile. Instead of answering his question, she asked, "Where is Gilberte?"

"She left because you were humming."

"Oh." Jaqueline paused, then began in a whisper, "If I tell you, you must not tell anyone else about this, not even Gilberte." Jaqueline eyed Blaise in feigned suspicion.

Blaise sighed. "I will keep your secret."

For a moment all of Jaqueline's pomp disappeared as she shyly held out the pile of papers. "I've been writing a comedy."

Blaise took the pile of papers and began to read the first page. "Jaquette, this is good. The words and the meter make for good poetry. How many acts are there?"

"Five," Jaqueline answered.

Blaise was impressed. "You should take it to Papa. I don't think he would mind if you used study time to write it."

"But I haven't been using study time...much. Suzanne and I have been working on it in the afternoons when we play. We're going to perform it for everyone May first when Florin's family visits us."

Blaise would have read more but Jaqueline snatched away the papers. She slid them into her grammar book and closed the cover with a snap. "It's a surprise," she said firmly.

Blaise was persistent. "I still think you should tell Papa what you're doing."

Jaqueline shrugged. "If you think Papa should know, why don't you tell him what you have been doing?"

"Oh that's different. Papa says mathematics fills the mind and gives so much satisfaction that..."

Jaqueline finished, "He is afraid once you started in mathematics you would never complete your other studies."

"But I like languages, too. There's a certain logic behind them, " countered Blaise.

Jaqueline laughed. "But I don't see Papa hiding grammar books from you."

Blaise straightened in his chair and said in his most authoritative voice, "Papa says a scholar must have the proper training and maturity to begin mathematics."

"Is that why you spend your free afternoons drawing lines and triangles on the floor!"

Blaise opened his book and pretended to read Cicero. Arguing with Jaquette was useless!

Jaqueline was about to say more when Madame

Delfaut bustled into the room. "Time to tidy up," she announced as she reached for the papers and books on the table. The children grabbed their books in an effort to save something before Madame Delfaut put it away. Blaise decided to appeal to their governess. "Madame Delfaut, do you think Papa would want to know if someone..." He paused and looked pointedly at Jaqueline. "If someone was pursuing some...er studies... that were not part of the usual curriculum?"

Madame paused from her perpetual motion and gave each of them a nod. "Yes to poetry, no to mathematics."

Blaise and Jaqueline looked at each other in amazement. Before they could ask Madame Delfaut how she knew, she continued in her quick clipped tones, "Please call your sister and father now. It is time for lunch."

Jaqueline and Blaise quickly obeyed, but they knew their discussion was not finished yet.

Later that evening, Blaise wrapped his bulky comforter around his shoulders. Silently, he slipped into Gilberte and Jaqueline's room. Jaqueline was ready for him and stealthily lit the tallow candle which they kept for such occasions. Gilberte opened their secret hoard of cashew nuts. As they always did, each of them took two nuts. They munched on their cashews while Gilberte opened the meeting in a solemn whisper. "A meeting has been called to discuss whether Monsieur Blaise Pascal should continue his study of mathematics, in particular, the area of geometry."

Jaqueline and Blaise exchanged glances. Apparently, Jaqueline did not want to mention her poetry.

Gilberte continued, "The esteemed Madame Delfaut seems to think geometry would be an unwise pursuit. Do I hear any rebuttal?"

Blaise took the floor. As he developed his argument, he spoke faster. "Papa, I mean, Monsieur Etienne Pascal, has always intended for his pupils to think. It was the very same Monsieur Etienne Pascal who said that `Geometry is the study of lines and their relationships,' the information which has been the basis of this study. Furthermore, Monsieur Etienne Pascal plans for Monsieur Blaise Pascal to study geometry one day anyway."

Jaqueline spoke up. "I say we call for a decision by vote."

Gilberte passed out one more nut to each participant. "Whole nut for yes, half nut for no," she intoned. "How many are in favor of Monsieur Blaise Pascal continuing his studies?" Three whole cashew nuts were placed in the middle of their circle.

Jaqueline spoke up. "I say we call for a decision by vote."

Gilberte passed out one more nut to each participant. "Whole nut for yes, half nut for no," she intoned. "How many are in favor of Monsieur Blaise Pascal continuing his studies?" Three whole cashew nuts were placed in the middle of their circle.

Chapter 4

The Youngest Scholar

On this particular Thursday in August of 1635, Blaise's father walked as a man with a purpose. Perhaps it would be better to say that Etienne Pascal strode to the meeting of the "Académie Libre." The "Académie Libre" was the weekly meeting of several mathematicians. It was loosely organized by Father Mersenne. The participants varied from week to week. Most of the members had other careers and studied mathematics and physics as a hobby. Many of the scholars lived in other cities and participated through letters. There were Desargues, the geometer from Lyons, Carcavy and Mydorge, who were lens makers, Roberval, professor of math at the College de France, Hardy, who was also a specialist in Oriental languages, and Le Pailleur, a close friend of Blaise's father.

When Etienne Pascal arrived, Le Pailleur was already there. Some people said Le Pailleur arrived early in order to sample the food. Whether this was true or not, it was certainly true that this self-taught scholar had a reputation for solving difficult problems. Etienne Pascal had a difficult problem.

"Le Pailleur, I'm glad you're the first to arrive. I need to talk to you about Blaise. He's been doing geometry."

Le Pailleur looked surprised, "Even after you hid all the books?" He caught his friend's hurt expression. "Why are you looking at me like that? I did not tell him anything. We all promised we would not talk to him about mathematics."

Blaise's father relaxed a little. "I found him drawing what we know as Euclid's 32nd proposition this morning. He had made up names to describe lines, circles, and the rest."

Le Pailleur whistled. "That means he figured out and built on the first 31 propositions!"

Pascal continued, "My plan was to hold him above his studies. I wanted to wait to introduce geometry until his mind was ready..."

Le Pailleur interrupted, "Pascal, you would be a fool to hold him back any longer. Obviously the boy is ready. Let him read all your books on the subject."

A slight cough from Father Mersenne made both men aware of his presence. "Excuse me," Father Mersenne began, "but I could not help overhearing your discussion. Pascal, bring your son with you when you come. I think he is developing into quite a thinker."

A smile began to spread across Etienne Pascal's face. He shook Father Mersenne's hand with more vigor than usual. "I will, Father. I will."

Jaqueline tugged on Blaise's hands. "Come on, Blaise, play the part of Rodrigue in El Cid."

Blaise freed himself from her grasp and returned to his book. It was the First Book of Euclid, which Papa had given him. Now that he was free to read books on mathematics, he read them during every free moment. Papa called mathematics a "sport". Blaise understood what his father meant. "Jaquette, can't you see that I'm busy?"

Jaqueline pouted. Though she had just celebrated her eleventh birthday, she still played the little sister role whenever it helped. "I should never have told you to let Papa know about your mathematics!"

Blaise looked up from his book long enough to say, "Well, I'm glad Papa knows about your writing. Look at all the good things that have happened. Papa even asked Monsieur Mondory to teach you acting."

Blaise had hoped for a quick end to their conversation, but at the mention of her acting instructor, Jaqueline had even more to say. "Oh yes! He is such a great actor. When he played Rodrigue he was so inspiring!"

Blaise was saved from having to re-enact the mighty Rodrigue by the appearance of Gilberte. She peeked into the room to announce that Papa was ready to go to the "Académie Libre" and was looking for Blaise.

Blaise quickly closed his book and ran to find his father. He had been looking forward to his first meeting with the Académie, but now he felt nervous. What would those fine scholars think of a thirteen-year-old boy attending such a meeting? His father seemed to understand Blaise's apprehension. He rested his hand on his son's shoulder for a moment. "The men you will meet are just like us. They enjoy searching for answers. I know they will give you much to think about."

Papa's words proved to be true. The father and son arrived in the middle of a heated discussion on the work of Galileo.

Le Pailleur was talking. "Galileo asserts that the earth moves around the sun as Copernicus explained. Galileo does not say this on a whim. He has seen the evidence with his own eyes through his telescopes."

Another man whom Blaise did not recognize began to speak. "I think the problem is that the Church would rather believe old myths and outdated theories by Aristotle. If experiments prove Aristotle's ideas, that is good; but if experiments prove Copernicus' ideas then the Church should change what she believes on this issue."

Le Pailleur followed up on the man's last statement. "Does that mean the Church might have to change other things...her views on God for instance?"

There was a long silence. Blaise's father spoke. "Are you asking whether truths of science can clash with the truths of the Bible?" He paused and allowed his colleagues to think about his question. Perhaps some were thinking how the wrong answer to such a question might result in condemnation by the Inquisition, as in Galileo's case. Etienne Pascal's answer to the question took them by surprise. "No gentlemen, the truths of the Bible are higher than the truths of science. Look more closely at the issue here. I trust that Galileo is a man who believes the Bible. He simply disagrees with Aristotle. Now, Aristotle was a scientist, not a writer of Holy Scripture. His ideas must be put to the test as all science must be. However, Christianity is true because of the authority of God, not by experiments."

Blaise listened intently to his father's speech. His father often said that science and faith were separate. But how could one know what was true? For the rest of the meeting Blaise barely paid attention. He was earnestly trying to sort out how he knew what he knew.

The discussion ended and the men began to disperse. Le Pailleur brought a stranger to meet Blaise and his father. "Please allow me to introduce my friend, Pierre de Fermat. He is a lawyer from Toulouse and studies mathematics as a hobby."

Blaise's father greeted him warmly. "I'm Etienne Pascal and this is my son, Blaise. My hobby is mathematics, too. For a moment, though, I thought it might be theology."

Fermat grinned. "I'm afraid that's too risky for my temperament. I will have to stick with mathematics."

The men shook hands once more and the Pascals left for home. Blaise waited until he had his father alone to ask him what Monsieur Fermat had meant by saying that theology was "risky."

Papa thought about his answer for a long time. When he began, he spoke slowly as though weighing each word. "Some people are afraid that they might be condemned by the Inquisition for stating what is actually the truth."

"But isn't the Inquisition part of the Church?"

Papa replied, "Yes, but in some places, like Italy, the Inquisition has begun to care less about the truth and more about politics."

Blaise was almost afraid to ask the next question. "Does that mean that God cares more about politics?"

Papa's face grew stern. "No," he said forcefully. "God

is always the same. It is men who change."

Blaise dug his hands into his pockets and tried to concentrate on what Papa said. Why did men change? One hand touched something - the rock Florin had given him. Somehow it was comforting to feel the sharp edges dig into his palms. At least there were some things that did not change.

Chapter 5

New Challenges

Though mathematics was not a dangerous pastime, by 1638 Papa's other pursuits had put him into great danger. When the family moved to Paris, Papa invested his wealth in bonds, which provided the family with a steady income. However, in March of 1638 the Royal Treasury decreased the interest on the bonds. Papa and other bondholders made a formal protest to Cardinal Richelieu, who was the real power behind the king. Richelieu responded by throwing three leaders of the protest into the Bastille prison.

That same night, Blaise was awakened by a firm grasp on his shoulder. In the dim candlelight he could see his father's face just a few inches from his own. Blaise thought how tired Papa looked.

Papa gripped Blaise's hand. "I've got to leave Paris," he said in a hoarse voice.

"Where are we going?" Blaise began to ask, but Papa raised his hand to silence his question.

"I will go alone. It would be too dangerous for the family. Madame Delfaut will be here. You and Gilberte are old enough to take care of Jaquette. Continue your studies, and if you need to get a message to me, you can send it through Florin's family in Clermont." Papa gave Blaise's hand a squeeze. His voice sank to a whisper. "God bless you, Son."

Blaise took Papa's parting words to heart and worked harder than ever at his studies. By this time he was a budding scientist and mathematician. His series of experiments on sound had led to a treatise on the subject. He had devoured all available works on mathematics. His restless mind constantly ranged the field for new challenges. His current work concerned conic sections, a thorny problem that had eluded scholars for centuries. At the meetings of the "Académie Libre" he was much sought after to help with other proofs in physics and mathematics. Scholars from Germany, England, and Italy wrote to him about their proofs. They would have been amazed to know that the mathematician they were consulting was only fourteen! Father Mersenne claimed that there had not been such a genius since Archimedes.

Blaise encouraged Jaqueline to write. She continued to distinguish herself as a poet. He accompanied her to Rouen where she won the "de la Tour" prize for one of her poems. At the award ceremony, Corneille, author of El Cid, wrote a few verses in her honor. Blaise wished Papa could have been there.

However, taking care of Jaqueline was more difficult than Blaise expected. Later that year Jaqueline contracted smallpox. Blaise called in the best doctors, but the vivacious young life was almost snuffed out. In agony, Blaise sent a message to Papa through Florin. Papa risked arrest in order to be at his little Jaquette's bedside.

Jaqueline lived, but her brush with death made her a more serious person. As she studied her face, disfigured by the pits of smallpox, she wrote:

> *These I accept, my sovereign Lord!*
> *As token seals that Thy blest Hand*
> *Would guard henceforth my innocence.* [1]

Blaise also became more serious. He began to read works by Montaigne and Descartes. Montaigne was the free-thinker of the day. In his Essais he analyzed himself and his feelings. He was skeptical of religion. Montaigne's skepticism was unsettling to Blaise, but he could not understand why. He read a few of the essays to Gilberte to get her opinion.

She sensed Blaise's uneasiness. "His views on religion bother you, don't they?" she asked.

Blaise shifted uncomfortably in his chair. He did not know what he thought. Papa revered religion as a truth beyond questioning, but Blaise did not know what he believed. He hesitantly framed his answer. "I guess he did not have to mention religion, but it is always our duty not to turn men from it."

Gilberte pretended to study her embroidery as she considered his answer for a moment. "I liked the essay by Descartes that you read me last week. He investigated reason instead of analyzing his own feelings. You must have liked that, Blaise."

Blaise gave her a wry smile. "Yes, I admire Descartes. He says that one should not accept any idea

---

1   Cailliet, Emile, Pascal: The Emergence of Genius (New York: Harper and Brothers, 1961) p 48.

until it can be proven. To Descartes that means dividing any problem into more basic parts until the truth of that part is self-evident. Then, by reason, one can build part upon part to prove the whole."

Gilberte gave a triumphant jab at her needlework. "And Descartes thinks he can prove the existence of God!"

Blaise shook his head as though trying to clear his mind. "I would have said the same thing last week," he replied. "But I've been reading more of Descartes' works. His philosophy works beautifully in mathematics and science, but the way Descartes tries to prove the existence of God using his new reason bothers me. Descartes seems to be quite willing to do away with God if another logical way for the world to be set in motion could be found."

Blaise lapsed into thought. What was it Papa always said? "There are some things you know by seeing and others that you know by believing." But believing in what? Blaise had a dim memory of Papa at the "Académie Libre" saying something about the Bible. What had he said?

During the long months of "Papa's exile", as Jaqueline liked to call it, Blaise kept himself busy. At fifteen he was the youngest member of the "Académie Libre". Since his first meeting with Fermat two years earlier, the two men had become good friends. Besides their common interest in mathematics, Fermat studied Greek literature as did Blaise. Fermat also wrote poetry. Blaise enjoyed experimenting with the use of words, but he ceded the realm of poetry to his sister and his friend.

One Thursday afternoon Blaise and Fermat were discussing conic sections. Blaise was talking fast as he did when he got excited. "Let's say you have two cones that are lined up so that their points touch. You can pass a plane through the cones in several ways and get many different shapes: circles, parabolas, ellipses, hyperbolas, and curved lines. There ought to be a way to explain the properties of conic sections using these simpler geometric figures."

Fermat nodded his head slowly. "I can picture the two cones end to end at their points, and even see what the intersection of a plane with them might look like. But how would you describe those figures? Euclid's geometry deals with planes, but how could you relate these to one another?"

Monsieur Desargues, who was an expert in geometry, interrupted, "Pascal, why don't you start from your knowledge of perspective and reduce the properties of conic sections to a small number of propositions?"

Blaise's face lit up. "Yes, why not?" He thought about conic sections for the rest of the meeting. He did not stop thinking about them that day, nor the next, nor the next. He worked on the problem constantly in the following months. Gradually the pieces of this new puzzle fell into place as Blaise developed a treatise on the subject. Unfortunately, the pursuit of answers was more satisfying to Blaise's soul than to his body. Blaise's health had never been good, and he had gotten used to neglecting it. Though he became more and more ill, he did not relax his pace.

One day Madame Delfaut cornered him in his study. "Your father would not want to see you like this," she said sternly.

Blaise broke away from his thoughts.

"What do you mean?"

Madame Delfaut continued. "You are wearing yourself out on your work. If you continue this way you won't be able to work. You need to rest."

Blaise rubbed his eyes and allowed his body to relax into the back of his chair. He did feel tired. "What do you suggest?"

Madame Delfaut smiled. "I had an idea that you might want to see Jaqueline's rehearsal. It's the first time she has been up since her bout with smallpox and Monsieur Mondory has her learning a new play."

Blaise agreed that would be a good idea and followed Madame to the front room. Jaqueline was already well into the play. She gathered fresh enthusiasm for her part when her audience entered. Blaise thoroughly enjoyed her performance.

Afterwards Madame Delfaut invited Monsieur Mondory to stay for dinner. They lingered over the meal, talking and laughing until late that night. For a few hours conic sections and planes were forgotten. When at last Monsieur Mondory left, Blaise returned to his work. With fresh resolve he put the finishing touches on his treatise, writing in his introduction:

If this matter is judged worthy of further study, we will try to push it to whatever point God will give us the strength to bring it.

Chapter 6

Inventor in Rouen

Jaqueline danced from side to side in impatience. "Blaise, please hurry!"

Blaise carefully set a glass upside down and gave it one last look. "I'm coming. I was just thinking of something."

Jaqueline laughed. "You're always thinking of something. Please put on this jacket. You want to look right for the Cardinal."

Blaise obligingly put on his jacket. As Jaqueline tried to straighten the large square collar of his shirt, Blaise thought to himself how hard it was to believe that only a year ago Jaqueline lingered close to death. Now she was more full of life than ever, and so much had happened.

Jaqueline had been invited to act in a play for Cardinal Richelieu. He was so impressed by her performance, that he offered to grant her any request. In a hastily composed verse, Jaqueline asked the Cardinal to pardon her father. All at once the family's lot had been reversed and Papa could come home. Now, Cardinal Richelieu was summoning the entire family to his fabulous palace in Rueil.

Blaise abandoned his reflections as Jaqueline began pulling on his arms. "Blaise! You said you would stop thinking! Come on!"

Blaise followed Jaqueline out the door. Papa and Gilberte were waiting in the coach. Blaise and Jaqueline climbed aboard, and the coach rattled down the cobblestone street. During the long ride Papa was quiet. Perhaps he was concerned about the meaning of this summons. Jaqueline, however, kept the conversation lively. She commented on everything she saw from the window. As a game she made poems to describe what she saw. Blaise and Gilberte enjoyed playing the game, too. As they passed a river dotted with several boats, Blaise called out:

> *Rivers are roads which move to and fro.*
> *They carry us whither we want to go.*

As they passed through the countryside, they spotted hares and squirrels. They played games counting the cows or sheep on the various farms that they passed. Blaise showed Gilberte and Jaqueline how to estimate large numbers accurately by counting a small group and multiplying by the number of groups. Before they knew it, the coach was rolling through the grand entrance of Cardinal Richelieu's palace.

A dignified man with a long moustache and a heavy gold chain around his neck greeted them. He explained that he was the steward. The Cardinal had asked him to make the guests welcome. After a tour of the grounds, he showed Blaise's family to their rooms.

Blaise was amazed by the lavish furnishings. Fine tapestries decorated all four walls. The plump comforter on his bed was turned back, revealing the smooth edge of the fine linen sheet. Blaise touched the silken tassel that hung from the corner of the bed, and ran his hand over the thick carpet.

Blaise wandered into the hallway. Heavy wooden furniture flanked the walls, and there were several mirrors, which dazzled Blaise. He had been exposed to court life before, but never anything like this!

During their stay, the family was treated like royalty. They enjoyed fine foods they had never tasted before, like the new vegetable called "asparagus." Blaise was the only one who liked it. They walked in the Cardinal's extraordinary gardens and sampled some of the beautifully bound books that were in his library. At night they listened to the music of violas and harpsichords wafting through their open bedroom windows. Despite all the luxuries, the high point of the visit was Papa's meeting with Cardinal Richelieu. The Cardinal seemed to have forgotten all past resentments. Instead, he appointed Papa to be "His Majesty's Deputy Commissioner in Upper Normandy."

At that time, Normandy was in a crisis. There was much hostility toward the King and the government due to the exorbitant taxes that were extracted from the citizens. Cardinal Richelieu needed someone to settle the stormy relations and reorganize the collection of taxes. Etienne Pascal's former job in Clermont and reputation as an honest and diplomatic man qualified him for the job. It was an honor that could not be refused.

Thus, early in the year of 1640, while the snow was still thick on the ground, the Pascal carriage could be seen making its way to Rouen in Normandy. Etienne Pascal proved to be all that the ailing government needed. He worked tirelessly to untangle the mess of tax laws and districts. He did not allow himself to sleep before 2:00 am more than six times during his first four months. The necessary computations, alone, were an overwhelming work load. Blaise began to help his father. Florin Périer also joined Papa's staff.

The more Blaise worked, the more he thought that there must be a better way to compute the mountain of numbers. He meticulously drew the plans for a calculating machine. After many revisions, he decided the machine was ready to be made. Numbers could be dialed on top of the machine, and cylinders inside the machine would be geared to turn one-tenth of a revolution for each revolution of the wheel to its right. The answer would be displayed on top of the machine through a series of slots.

The job of making the machine, however, was more difficult than Blaise had anticipated. He tirelessly assembled and perfected the parts he needed. He experimented with using wood, ivory, leather, ebony and metal. After two years of persevering at his task, he finished the first model of the calculating machine. It was in a metal case a little smaller than a loaf of bread. He could use it to add, subtract, multiply, and divide. Blaise's father could perform his calculations in a fraction of the time it used to take. Blaise continued to improve the machine and would make more than fifty models during the next ten years.

During the two years that Blaise worked on the

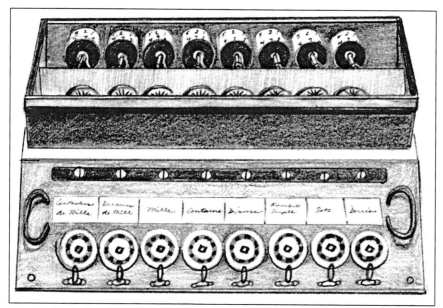

The Calculating Machine invented by Blaise.

machine, Gilberte and Florin got married and moved to Clermont. When the machine was finally constructed, Blaise could not wait to show it to them. At last the day came when Gilberte and Florin visited. Blaise demonstrated his machine for them. Gilberte was impressed, but she could not resist the opportunity to tease Blaise. "It does seem a pity," she said, "to reduce a science, that was totally dependent on the mind, to a machine. Now you can make all the calculations with accuracy without any use of reason! It looks like you are no longer needed."

Blaise did not take her teasing well. He retorted, "Madame, you are mistaken. We have not even begun to tap the resources of the human mind."

Gilberte caught something different in the tone of her brother's voice. She studied him carefully, then softly said, "Beware of pride, Blaise."

   Blaise blushed. He knew she was right, but he increasingly felt trapped by emotions he did not understand. He remembered how proud he had felt when Descartes-the great Descartes- complimented him for his work on conic sections. He admitted to himself that he enjoyed the praise of his colleagues at the "Académie Libre." Their admiration drove him to work harder and harder. With each new conquest he enjoyed the acclaim more. Where would this end?

Chapter 7

A God-Shaped Vacuum

It was six years since Blaise's family moved to Rouen. The years had been filled with hard work. The people of Rouen had come to respect and love their Deputy Commissioner. He was an honest man. They noticed approvingly how he and his family were regular and respectful in their religious practice. He had done a fine job of restructuring their tax laws and avoiding an uprising. One New Year's Day the town presented him with a purse of silver pieces coined especially in his honor. As the throne passed from Louis XIII to the boy king, Louis XIV, the simple citizens of Rouen rejoiced to see that their Deputy Commissioner kept his post. They increasingly sought his help in a variety of matters that touched their lives.

On an icy January morning of 1646 there was a loud knocking on the Pascal door. Papa and Blaise paused in their discussion of the new "Torricelli experiment," and Blaise sprang to answer the door. A man stood on the front step. His face was white and he was trying to catch his breath. He managed to say, "Quick. A duel. Monsieur Pascal must come at once."

Blaise helped his father throw on his overcoat and held the massive door against the wind, as Papa hastily stepped out onto the ice-glazed front steps. Suddenly Papa's feet flew out from under him. Blaise heard a snap as of bones popping apart, and time seemed to stand still. The wind whipped through Blaise's thin shirt as he lurched to his father's side. He felt like he was moving in slow motion. He kneeled beside his father. "Papa, are you hurt?" There was no answer from his father.

With the help of the man, Blaise lifted his father's unconscious form to the couch in the front room. Madame Delfaut appeared immediately and ran to get the smelling salts. Blaise himself hurried out to find a doctor.

By noon, he had found two men who were trained in medicine. Their names were Adrien and Jean Deschamps. The two brothers were noblemen who had become monks. They served others by using their knowledge of medicine.

The Deschamps carefully tended Blaise's father. They found that Etienne Pascal had dislocated his hip. "He will need constant care for a while," Adrien Deschamps explained to Blaise. "In our service as monks, we are prepared to stay with you if you like."

Blaise and Papa agreed that it would be best to have the men remain in their home. Madame Delfaut bustled around the house making the necessary preparations for their stay.

In the days that followed, Blaise came to admire these two men. They cared for his father with great skill, yet they were humble and eager to serve. What a contrast their modesty was to his own pride.

One night Blaise could not sleep. He went to his father's room. Adrien Deschamps was still there keeping watch over his sleeping patient.

"I'll watch him for a while," Blaise whispered.

The monk smiled and nodded. He retired to his room, which was only a few steps away.

Blaise sat next to his father and studied his face. How frail he looked. Blaise's thoughts seemed particularly active tonight. He liked to make mental notes and store them for later examination. Tonight he wrote in his mind:

When I think about the short duration of my life, it seems to be lost in the time that came before me and will come after me...

Who has put me here? By whose order and plan have this place and time been given to me?

Scenes of Papa talking about God flickered through his mind. Blaise continued his mental notes:

Between us and hell or heaven there is nothing but life, which is the most fragile thing in the world.

Blaise smiled sadly as he thought of how life is so much like one of Jaqueline's plays.

The last act is tragic, no matter how happy all the rest of the play is. At the end a little earth is thrown upon our head, and that is the end forever.

But did it have to be that way? Was what he could see all that there was?

Why is my knowledge limited?

Blaise thought of how Descartes wrote that man could prove the existence of God, but that did not satisfy Blaise. Did Descartes really have faith when he was so proud as to think he could judge whether God was truly there? With the monks it was different. They had faith...

It seems that nature testifies to God some, but not completely.

I envy those whom I see living in the faith with so much carelessness. They make bad use of a gift which I would use so differently.

Blaise felt empty. The ancient scholars defined a vacuum as pure emptiness. To Blaise it seemed as though there were a big vacuum in the middle of his soul. Again he asked himself, Who has put me here?

Blaise was startled to hear the creak of a door behind him. It was Jean Deschamps coming in to take his turn at the bedside. He was surprised to see Blaise.

"Couldn't sleep?" he asked softly.

Blaise shook his head.

At that moment Adrien Deschamps appeared in the doorway. The brothers exchanged quick glances. Then Jean turned to Blaise and motioned him out of the room. In the hallway, he said, "Come, let's get a cup of tea. Adrien will watch."

Blaise marvelled that Jean was willing to give up his sleep for the sake of a conversation. He wondered if Jean knew how desperately he wanted to talk with him. Blaise followed Jean to the kitchen. He watched quietly as the monk made the tea.

At last Blaise broke the silence. "How long do you think it will be before Papa is better?"

"Perhaps three months, perhaps five," Jean answered.

"It's good of you to help him." Blaise continued.

Jean sat down in front of Blaise and gave him a searching look. "We try to ease physical suffering. We also care about the deeper suffering of the spirit."

Blaise did not say anything, but Jean seemed to understand.

Humbly the monk began an explanation. "Blaise, have you heard of `the grace of God'?" He did not wait for Blaise's answer. "The Bible clearly tells us that our sin prevents us from knowing God. However, God sent his Son, our Lord Jesus Christ, to take the punishment that our sin deserved. That is grace. A gift. By faith we can accept God's gift. Then we spend the rest of our lives getting to know God."

Blaise almost choked on his words. "God can be known?"

The monk simply replied, "The Bible says we can know Him."

Blaise straightened in his chair. "I want to have faith," he declared.

Jean said, "The Bible says, `He who seeks shall find.' I will pray for you that you will find what you seek."

He rose to leave, but Blaise stopped him. "Wait. Where should I seek?"

The monk smiled. "In the Bible."

Chapter 8

A New Passion

The next day Blaise began searching for a copy of the Bible. He asked Papa if he had a copy of the Bible. Papa had been lying listlessly in bed. At Blaise's question he raised his head, and a gleam of interest kindled in his eyes. "Why do you want to know, son?"

Blaise shrugged and tried to act nonchalant. "I guess I just wanted to read for myself what it says. I've been listening all these years to what the priests read."

Blaise's father nodded approvingly. "That's right. Your mother and I used to feel the same way. Somewhere around here we have the Bible in Latin. Look on the shelf behind Euclid."

Blaise followed his father's directions and soon found himself holding a very dusty volume in his hands.

The entire project seemed to enliven Papa. For the first time in weeks he actually made a teasing remark. He smiled and said, "I can't believe Madame Delfaut did not banish that dust all these years!"

Blaise felt a growing excitement inside himself. Gingerly he opened the cover of the Bible and scanned row upon row of words that filled the pages. Here were the answers he was looking for; he only had to study.

In the days that followed, Blaise poured over the Bible. With each new discovery, he ran to Papa's room where the monks were usually in attendance.

"Look, here in Romans 3:23 it says that `all have sinned'."

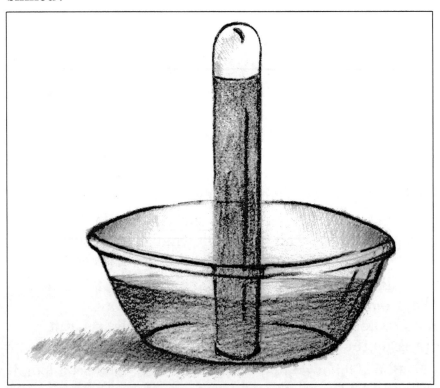

Blaise decided to find out what was in the top of the tube in the Torricelli experiment.

Or another time, "Papa, Brother Jean, did you ever read in Isaiah 59:2 where it says 'Your sins have hid his face from you...'?"

Or again, "Brother Adrien, Romans 5:8 says 'God commendeth his love for us, in that, while we were yet sinners, Christ died for us.'"

At last the day came when he read in John 1:12: "But as many as received Him to them He gave power to become sons of God, even to them that believe on his name." Blaise bowed his head and prayed, "Lord, I have sought you all my life. Now I want to believe. Please make me your child."

Blaise was so excited that he had to explain it all to Jaqueline. For the next week they talked of nothing but God and Jesus Christ. The words of the Bible, which they discussed, touched Jaqueline's soul. She told Blaise that she felt as though she had finally put a name to a dear friend's face. She, too, became a child of God.

During Blaise's frequent visits to Papa's bedside, he often found his father heatedly talking with the Deschamps brothers about a particular section of the Bible which Blaise had read. It was from Ephesians 2:8 and read: "For by grace are ye saved through faith; and that not of yourselves: it is the gift of God: not of works, lest any man should boast."

One afternoon, not long after Jaqueline came to believe in Christ, Blaise went to see his father. Papa was in a talkative mood and wanted to hear what Blaise had been reading in the Bible. Blaise had only spoken a few words, when Papa interrupted him. "That's exactly what I have a problem with," he began. "How can we be saved as a gift? It would not be fair to the man who has been good all his life if he was saved the same way as a criminal."

Blaise was taken back by his father's intensity. The idea of being saved as a gift had been such a relief to Blaise. He had felt so empty. If God had not revealed himself through the Bible, and filled that God-shaped vacuum as a gift, Blaise felt sure he would have spent his life in uncertainty and despair. Yet Papa was different. All his life he had tried to do the right thing. He had raised three children: taking them to church, always telling them that God is true.... Perhaps he had not yet come to terms with the need for a Savior.

Blaise fumbled in his Bible for a passage that he had recently read. "I think there is something here that might interest you." He paused a moment while he found the right spot, then slowly he began to read the account in Luke of Jesus dying on the cross. He read about one of the robbers who was being crucified with Jesus and how he believed. He read how Jesus promised the robber that he would go to heaven. When Blaise finished, he looked up and saw that there were tears in his father's eyes.

"I understand now." he said.

Blaise delighted in his new faith, and enjoyed discussing the Bible with his family. He also found a renewed zeal for his scientific pursuits. His father and he had witnessed a demonstration of the new "Torricelli experiment". Torricelli was an Italian physicist, and his idea was simple. Take a glass tube that is closed on one end. Fill it with a fluid, such as mercury. Then turn it upside-down in a bowl of the same liquid. The liquid would fall only part way down the tube, leaving a space at the top of the tube. As of yet, no one knew what was in that space or why it was there. Blaise decided to find out.

Meticulously, he designed his experiments and the equipment he would need. He performed each experiment with great precision. As his father had trained him, he recorded and evaluated each trial. He made a myriad of variations of Torricelli's experiment. He changed the fluids, trying mercury, water, red vinegar, oil, and many others. He changed the sizes, lengths, and shapes of the vessels used. At about this time, Gilberte and Florin came for a visit. Blaise immediately enlisted Florin's help in his research.

Blaise set a case of red bottles on the steps and wiped the sweat from his eyes. He turned to Florin, who was just putting the last case on the pile. "I thought the shopkeeper's eyes were going to pop out of his head when we ordered all these cases."

His friend had his hands on his hips, and was breathing heavily from the exertion. "Blaise, tell me why we need all this red vinegar."

Blaise assumed the air of a magician about to produce something amazing. "Come with me and I will show you."

Florin followed Blaise around the side of the house where a heavy canvas covered a long object that ran the length of several houses. With a flourish, Blaise threw back one end of the canvas to reveal the longest glass tube Florin had ever seen.

"For this," Blaise said.

Florin's eyes widened. "We are going to put all that vinegar in that...that tube? How long is it?"

"Forty-six feet long," Blaise replied.

Florin began to look worried. "We are going to need help! There is no way we can do this ourselves."

Blaise chuckled. "Did you think I was going to hold it on end while you climbed up the ladder and poured the vinegar in?"

Florin laughed sheepishly, but he could not hide his skepticism.

"Some men from the shipyard are going to help me lash it to a mast and get it into position," Blaise explained.

"Into position?"

"Yes. At first I want it to be upright and submersed about a foot in a tub of water. That will leave forty-five feet of tube above the surface of the water. Then I want to tilt it to various heights."

Florin shook his head. "You're incredible. Crazy, but incredible."

Blaise smiled and rubbed his hands together. "Let's get started."

It took all day to get the tube filled and set up in position. The men from the shipyard gaped in amazement at the fantastic length of the tube. When Blaise started measuring the height of the liquid left when the tube was upright in the tub of water, they lit their pipes and watched him as though he were performing an astonishing feat. For years afterwards, when the nights were long and the sea was quiet, many a sailor would gather his shipmates and tell them tales of "Le grand Pascal" and his wondrous experiments.

Next, Blaise had them tilt the mast. With a gurgle, that almost surprised the sailors into dropping the mast, the liquid established a new height in the tube. Blaise's excitement grew as he measured the new height in relation to both the length of the tube that it filled and its height from the ground. After the last measurement, he let out a whoop of triumph. "Florin, when the tube was inclined, the liquid rose to the same distance from the ground that it measured when upright: thirty-two feet."

Blaise did not wait for Florin to respond. He gestured wildly to his helpers. "Look, I'm going to mark thirty-two feet on this wall here. Can you tilt the mast so that the tip is exactly thirty-two feet off the ground?"

The men grabbed hold of the mast and ropes that held it in place, and lowered it into position. This time they were ready for the gurgling sound as the liquid rushed into the tube and filled it completely.

Blaise was almost delirious with joy as he measured the column of pure red vinegar at the top of the tube, all thirty-two feet of it. The remaining thirteen feet of pink fluid at the bottom was vinegar which had mixed with water in the tub before being drawn back into the tube.

"Florin, do you know what this means?"

"Yes," quipped Florin, "We have thirty-two feet of vinegar."

Blaise could not rest until he had tried the entire experiment over and over again. As Blaise analyzed the results, a new idea tantalized him. What if the space at the top of the tube was a vacuum? Ever since Aristotle, scholars had taken it for granted that vacuums could not exist. But what if they could? Blaise tore at the problem like a lion tearing at its prey. He designed totally new experiments with new equipment. He used bellows, syphons and syringes. When an instrument was not available, he invented it.

One such devise was a syringe with a precisely fitted piston. It was the first pneumatic device and led to the discovery of "Pascal's Law". Pascal's law states that when

the pressure on a liquid or gas in a container is increased
or decreased at one point, the change in pressure takes
place equally throughout. During his life, Blaise would
invent a myriad of practical uses for this idea. Today, we
use it for hundreds of gadgets that affect our daily lives.
This "change in pressure" is used to drive machinery, run
elevators, pump air for organs, activate the brakes on cars,
and to power jacks, pneumatic hammers, and torque
wrenches.

As Blaise energetically tackled the problem of the
vacuum, however, he was not yet aware of the
significance of his work. As the answers emerged, he
carefully built fact upon fact until he proved the existence
of the vacuum. Only the task of describing and publishing
his research remained. As he prepared the manuscript,
he wondered what kind of impact his findings would
have.

Meanwhile, Blaise's passion for the truth about God
led him to another type of research. While Gilberte and
Florin were visiting, he had a difficult time explaining
the Bible to them. This impasse forced him to study more
than ever. The monks recommended the sermons of one
particular church leader who preached from the Bible.
Blaise attended the sermon every week. He gathered
every bit of information he could that would help
Gilberte and Florin to understand the truth. Sometimes
Gilberte would laugh and say, "You're trying too hard,
Blaise." However, Blaise could not rest while his sister
and brother-in-law were ignorant of the truth. He kept
trying. Finally, the day came when Blaise burst into the
house yelling, "Gilberte and Florin have believed!"

Another day an entirely different piece of news sparked
Blaise's excitement. "Jaquette, did you hear the news?

Friar Forton has been appointed to a church in Normandy!"

Jaqueline wrinkled her nose. "Is he the one who says Jesus was not of the blood of Mary, but was a different substance?"

"The very one! He attacks the Bible at every point and substitutes his own myths."

"How can he do that?" queried Jaqueline.

"He thinks he can set up a higher authority than the Bible_himself!" Blaise was angry. His words shot out like quickly fired bullets. "This situation must be corrected. I've asked two of my friends to go with me to see Friar Forton. The Bible says to go to the wrong-doer in private first. Perhaps he will change his opinions."

Later that week, the three young men went to see Friar Forton. If they had hoped to resolve the problem easily, they were disappointed. The old friar refused to change his views and said that he believed many other ideas that were not in the Bible.

The next week the young men took the matter to the Archbishop. At first they could not get an appointment with him. They were undaunted, however, and tried again the following week. The issue was slightly complicated by the fact that Blaise's father held an important post in Normandy, the place of Friar Fortons's appointment. In the end, the sincerity of the three men won them a chance to see the Archbishop. They impressed the archbishop with their zeal for the truth, and Friar Forton was forced to change his views.

Blaise had no time to sit back and enjoy the victory, however. Soon he would enter an even larger and more dangerous battlefield.

The experiment with a tall glass tube led to the first scientific observance of a controlled vacuum. The data from this experiment led to the science of hydrolics as well as the syringe and many other useful daily devices.

Chapter 9

Weighty Issues

A few weeks after the Friar Forton problem was solved, Blaise's health suddenly worsened. His legs began to ache, and his headaches spiked to new heights of pain. Blaise tried playing tennis and taking long horseback rides to improve his health, but nothing helped. One afternoon he returned from a horseback ride through the beautiful apple orchards of Normandy. His mind felt refreshed, but the pains in his head and legs were almost unbearable. When he awoke the next morning, he had lost the use of his legs. Blaise sought the advice of his friends, Adrien and Jean Deschamps. They recommended that Blaise get some rest. Blaise had received this advice before, but he found himself saying, "I can't stop now. The glass blowers just finished the scalene siphon with the fifty feet and forty-five feet legs."

Brother Adrien was stern. "Blaise, you need your rest. You must be content with only accomplishing what God gives you the strength to do."

This was a totally new idea to Blaise. He winced inwardly as he realized how important his work was to him. His research established his reputation, and his reputation was his source of self-worth and pride. He was ashamed to consider how much of his old pride he had, despite his new faith.

The monk continued, "You need to get help from the doctors in Paris. Our medicine covers only the simple things."

Blaise knew the monks were being humble. They had cured his father with great skill. If they could not help him, could any doctor restore him to health?

Jaqueline accompanied Blaise to Paris. Papa would follow after he retired from his post the next year. Their curate from Rouen recommended the sermons by Monsieur Singlin at the Church of Port-Royal. The Christians of Port-Royal were very devoted to their faith. The Port-Royal community maintained a school, a convent and a retreat area for scholars. They took the Bible seriously. They recognized its authority over all parts of their lives as had Augustine and the Bible's more recent champion, Cornelius Jansen.

Cornelius Jansen was a bishop in Ypres, Belgium, who had written in support of such doctrines as grace and the sovereignty of God. The French called believers who agreed with him "Jansenists." Besides their belief in the Bible's authority, Jansenists were known for their high level of moral, ethical and intellectual standards. Their school was famous for its excellent scholarship. It was also the only school in France whose students learned the Greek language before they learned Latin. They wanted to prepare the students to read the New Testament in the original Greek.

Port-Royal had two locations: Port-Royal of Paris and Port-Royal of the Country. The country location was the original home of the convent. It was located close to marshlands which became an unhealthy place for a few months each year. During those seasons the convent was moved to Paris for a few months. Blaise and Jaqueline attended church at the Port-Royal of Paris. Both Pascals were challenged by Monsieur Singlin's sermons which they heard there. Jaqueline told Blaise, "One could reasonably be a nun in a place like that."

Blaise often lingered after the sermons. In this way he met Monsieur de Rebours who was Monsieur Singlin's assistant. The two men made an appointment to talk together. Blaise eagerly awaited the day of their meeting. When at last he sat in Monsieur de Rebours' study, Blaise felt shy. He tried to cover his awkwardness by asking the learned man a question.

"Sir," he began, "Could common sense lead to the gateway of believing?"

Monsieur de Rebours hesitated to answer, so Blaise quickly added, "In other words, could common sense make a person interested in studying the Bible? I don't mean to say that it were possible to use common sense to judge whether God is true or not."

Monsieur de Rebours placed the fingers of his hands together and studied Blaise for a moment. "So you have

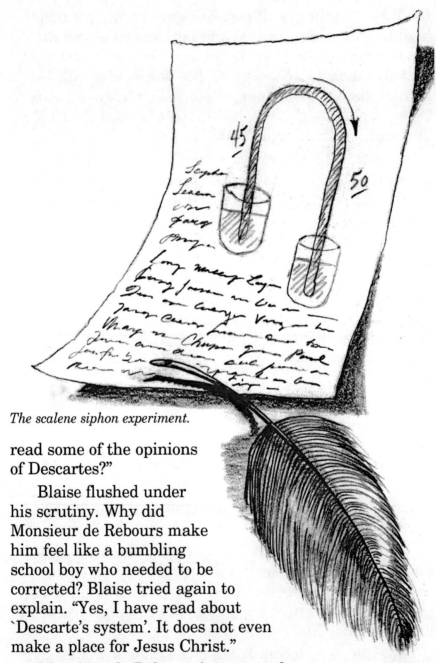

The scalene siphon experiment.

read some of the opinions of Descartes?"

Blaise flushed under his scrutiny. Why did Monsieur de Rebours make him feel like a bumbling school boy who needed to be corrected? Blaise tried again to explain. "Yes, I have read about `Descarte's system'. It does not even make a place for Jesus Christ."

Monsieur de Rebours interrupted. "Blaise, if you want to use common sense as the basis for your own faith, I can only give you this advice: humble yourself."

Blaise opened his mouth to defend himself, but Monsieur de Rebours stayed him with his hand. "Now let us pray. We will talk again another day."

Blaise quietly left Monsieur de Rebours' study, but inside he felt as though he were exploding. He longed to make this pious man understand his question. The only answer Monsieur had given him was humble yourself! Blaise thought to himself, "That would have been my advice to Descartes. Do I need that advice, too?" Monsieur de Rebours' message gave him much to think about.

Providentially, Blaise had a lot of time to think. The doctors in Paris ordered him to stop all work, but he chafed under the restrictions. He had just published the summary of his work with the vacuum and was eager to write the full report. As Blaise lay in bed, he thought his impatience was a worse trial than the headaches and paralysis. One afternoon, when he could stand it no longer, he pulled out his copy of the vacuum summary to read it one more time. He asked himself, "Was I being humble when I wrote this preface to the experiment?"

We should regulate differently the extent of our respect according to the distinction between authority and reason.

Blaise had to admit that it sounded like he was lecturing his reader. "But," he thought to himself, "I have to say it. People need to understand that facts are only as strong as the strength of their proof." He remembered the hours Papa spent teaching Latin grammar. Jaqueline would grow impatient with following the grammar rules, but Papa would take her back to the grammar book and show her the rules. He would tenderly remind her, "When writing in Latin you must use the facts found in the Latin grammar book." When Papa discussed laws with his friends, it was the same. They would quote laws that were recorded in books and say, "The King must do such and such because that is written in the laws of France." Likewise, Blaise and Papa had often discussed how Christians found real facts in the Bible because God wrote it. None of those facts could be learned by experimenting. What could be known was found in books written by those who had authority to state the facts. Blaise read the next part of his preface to the experiment:

> *It is quite otherwise with subjects accessible to sense or reasoning. Geometry, arithmetic, music, physics, and all the sciences subject to experiment and reason must be added to if they are to become perfect.*

Blaise nodded to himself and said aloud, "Here we know facts are true by reason and experiment. But is it pride to use reason and experiment?" Monsieur de Rebours' words echoed in his mind: "Humble yourself." Blaise forced himself to read the rest of the preface:

> *The clearing up of this difference should make us pity the blindness of those who use only authority, instead of reason or experiment, as proof in physics. It should fill us with horror at the wickedness of others who use only reason, instead of the authority of Scriptures, in theology. The ancients were right to say that nature did not permit the vacuum, because all their experiments had always led to that conclusion. However, if the new experiments had*

*been known to them, perhaps they would have
affirmed what they had reason to deny... They
meant to speak of nature only as they knew it.*

Blaise smoothed the papers on his lap and bowed his
head. "O Lord," he whispered, "Help me to do the right
thing. I want to seek the truth."

★ ★ ★ ★ ★ ★ ★ ★ ★ ★

Blaise's inner turmoil drove him to a deeper study of
the Bible. The more he read, the more troubled he was
by what he should do with his life. He believed in God in
a time and place where most men who had made such
commitments confined themselves to monasteries or
chose the priesthood. Would God want him to give up
Science? Jaqueline was experiencing a similar turmoil in
regards to her poetry. Often they discussed these issues.

One afternoon Jaqueline was reading the Bible as
she sat next to Blaise's bed. "The Bible says in 1 John
2:16 that `All that is in the world, the lust of the flesh,
the lust of the eyes, and the pride of life, is not of the
Father, but is of the world.' I want to be of the Father
and not of this world, don't you, Blaise?"

"Are you saying we should give up everything?"
Blaise asked. "Consider the parable of the talents. Aren't
we supposed to use our gifts for God?"

"But what if that means the gifts God has given us in
a spiritual sense, like peace, kindness and faith?"
Jaqueline countered.

Blaise was thoughtful. He did not share Jaqueline's
growing conviction that one needed to give up one's work
in the world in order to live as a Christian. "I need to

study this more," he said.

And study, he did. Blaise purchased the Bible in Greek so that he could read it in the original language. He also began to study Saint Augustine's works. Saint Augustine had been one of the most learned men of his day- the waning years of the Roman Empire. He had given up his work and its prestige in order to devote himself to studying the Bible and explaining it to others. Yet he felt that science was an acceptable pursuit.

Blaise explained to his sister, "Augustine taught that it is a waste of time to study science or to seek knowledge merely for the pleasure of it. But he also said it can be a sincere quest for truth in order to seek God and His glory. I agree."

Jaqueline shook her head. "You know that science has always been a sport to you. Are you going to change now?"

Blaise knew she was right. "I'm trying to change from the inside out, but it's hard."

Chapter 10

Of Truth and Error

Meanwhile, Blaise's conclusions about the vacuum fell on the scientific and philosophical community like a bomb. Scientists, like Torricelli, hailed it as a triumph of the experimental method. Philosophers, who narrowly adhered to Aristotle's theories about the world, were scandalized. To them, Aristotle carried equal authority with the Bible. Aristotle's works were the ultimate authority on science just as the Bible was the ultimate authority on religion. In fact, some of them would sooner question the Bible's authority, than the authority of Aristotle. A large number of these philosophers were influential leaders in the Church. Blaise was in a dangerous situation.

The forces behind Aristotle appointed a scholar called Father Noel to defend their side. He belonged to the same group that controlled the Inquisition. This group, or "Society" as they called themselves, was also responsible for spreading a lot of false information about the Bible. Like Descartes, they thought man, himself, could determine the truth about God, even if his ideas contradicted the Bible. Blaise had to fight his battle on two fronts: defending the experimental method on one hand, and the authority of the Bible on the other.

Father Noel dug into his task with all the venom he could muster. He attacked Pascal for contradicting Aristotle's philosophy, which had been accepted for hundreds of years. He appealed to the authority of Descartes who did not agree with Pascal. Wasn't Descartes a much more worthy scientist than Pascal?

From his bed, Blaise responded with a carefully reasoned reply:

One should never make a judgement unless:

1) *it is so obvious to the senses or reason that it is a principle or axiom, or*

2) *it may be deduced as an infallible and necessary consequence of a principle or axiom.*

Otherwise, it is merely an "idea," and not a fact.

Blaise explained how both he and Aristotle had "ideas," but only his own "ideas" were proven by the experimental method. He built his case methodically: first establishing the facts, then building on them. He could not resist correcting his opponent on his sloppy religious beliefs:

We put faith only into those truths which are revealed by the Holy Spirit in the Bible.

Blaise knew in a battle over religious points that he could point to God's words in the Bible to establish the truth. Equally well, he knew he could point to experiments which could be seen and touched to establish the truth in the scientific area.

Father Noel responded by conceding that vacuums do exist; however, he criticized Pascal for his religious beliefs. At that point Blaise asked his father to write on his behalf. His father wrote:

Blaise could not reply to these words, nor address his reply to you, unless in rebuffing your unexpected insults he might incite further discourses of a similar nature. He wanted to practice the Gospel precept, namely, to make our complaints and brotherly corrections directly to those who have given us grounds for them. He thought it more fitting to beg me, as he has indeed done, to take pains to practice this same Gospel precept myself, in making you understand his just complaints.

Etienne Pascal went on to quote the Bible in defense of his points.

Despite the criticism, Blaise was buoyed by a sense of accomplishment. God had given him a flexible mind that was quick to dream of possibilities. The possibilities for his work on the vacuum were endless: forecasting the weather, calculating altitudes, correcting thermometers, the study of the equilibrium of liquids and gases, a well that was powered by the "change in pressure", and a hydraulic press. Blaise saw another fascinating possibility. One last frontier remained to be explained before his work would be complete.

"To tell you frankly what I think, Florin, I can't believe that nature, which is not alive, is capable of `horror'. `Horror' presupposes a soul capable of feeling." Though Blaise was confined to bed, he waved his arms and spoke hurriedly as though there was not enough time for all that he wanted to say.

Florin was making a rare visit to Paris. His work as a councilor in Clermont usually kept him too busy for visiting. However, this time his work actually took him to Paris, and he was able to visit the Pascal home. Florin queried, "If you don't think nature abhors a vacuum, then what accounts for the space in the top of the tube?"

Blaise leaned forward and tried to speak slowly for emphasis. "What if the mercury column was formed, not because of the `pull' of the vacuum, but because of the `push' of the outside air on the pool of mercury?"

"How could that be?" asked Florin

Blaise continued, "I've already shown that the vacuum had no weight. What if the outside air did have weight?"

Florin brightened. "I see. Then the force of the air pushing down would cause the mercury to rise in the tube until its own weight was balanced with the air."

Blaise began talking quickly again. "I've designed an experiment to test this idea. It simply involves performing Torricelli's experiment at different altitudes. Everything would remain the same except the weight and pressure of the air."

Blaise's enthusiasm was contagious. Florin chuckled. "I don't see why the experiment you propose can't be done. It would really knock down those old ideas about a vacuum."

"I'll let you know how it goes,"Blaise promised. "As soon as the doctor lets me get out of bed."

Florin left, and Blaise waited for the doctor to arrive. He was eager to show the doctor how he could get around with the use of crutches. More than anything else, Blaise wanted to perform the experiment he had so carefully designed.

Blaise thought of Jaqueline's words: "Patience is a fruit of the Holy Spirit," but he could not yet accept that. Instead he kept asking God, "Why this illness? Why now?" Despite the doctor's prescriptions, purges, bleedings, and wrapping Blaise's legs in bandages soaked in brandy, Blaise was not improving. He rarely had even one hour free from pain. Nevertheless, he was driven to complete his work on the vacuum.

At last the doctor arrived. After examining Blaise, he shook his head. "I've done everything I can do, Monsieur Pascal. You must rest. Trying to walk with crutches will only set you back."

Blaise was bitterly disappointed. That night he slept fitfully. Finally he lit a candle and reached for the book that lay open next to his bed. The page of the book was weighted with a black rock. (Florin had laughed when he saw it there earlier in the day. "I can't believe you still have this," he teased.) Blaise took the small, hard piece of the mountain in his hand. It's solidness was always a comfort to him, but tonight it reminded him of something else. He extinguished the candle and went back to sleep. In the morning he had a solution.

Several months passed, and Blaise was still confined to bed. Early one morning there was a knock at the door. Jaqueline answered it. It was a messenger with a letter. Jaqueline studied the address on the letter for a moment, then stopped by Blaise's door to see if he was awake. At the sound of her footsteps, he awoke. "Oh, I'm sorry to waken you, Blaise, but this letter just arrived from Florin."

At her words, Blaise quickly sat up in bed. "Let me see it." He could hardly contain his excitement. He tore open the letter and began to read it. Suddenly, he let out a whoop. "Jaqueline, it worked! It worked!" He grabbed the paper, ink and pen that lay next to his bed and began to write furiously.

"What worked?" queried Jaqueline.

Blaise stopped writing long enough to say, "The experiment on the vacuum. Florin performed it for me at the Puy de Dome. Perfect place for it.... And it worked. It worked!"

Jaqueline shook her head in bewilderment. "I guess that means you won't be needing to eat or sleep or rest for a few days?" she asked pointedly.

Blaise grinned at her. "I'm in bed aren't I?" He dipped his pen in the ink well and rapidly scattered line after line of words across the page.

Chapter 11

Full Consolation

Gradually Blaise's health improved, and his spirits rose like the column of mercury in the Torricelli tube. He visited with Gilberte and Florin's family for a while. It felt good to be back in the town where he had spent the first seven years of his life. He looked fondly upon the sturdy town walls encircled by the homely vegetable gardens of the villagers. The Puy de Dome still kept its watch over the town. Its rounded summit was shrouded in mist.

Blaise once more had the freedom to pursue his scientific interests. He perfected the barometer, made pumps, clocks, gears, and winches. Gilberte was fascinated with a little clock he designed to be worn around the wrist. Blaise amused his nieces and nephews with his unusual time piece. He might have tarried in Clermont longer, but he received an urgent message from Jaqueline that she needed him at home.

Blaise wondered what could be the matter. Papa had
retired that spring of 1648. Surely Papa could take care of
things. Another possibility gripped Blaise with fear. Could
it be that their lives were in danger from the Fronde? The
Fronde was a rebellion led by the nobles against the king.
It started when the Parliament of Paris revolted against
the king's tax policies. In the past the skirmishes between
the two sides had not seemed to affect everyday life. But
what if Papa was in danger? After all, he had been Deputy
Commissioner in Normandy...

Blaise did everything he could to get home quickly.
Despite the coachman's effort, it took two days before the
coach arrived in Paris. Stepping down from the coach,
Blaise noticed with some relief that the exterior of his
home appeared peaceful. He mounted the steps to the
front door as fast as his cane would allow. Madame
Delfaut opened the door even as he was reaching for the
handle. "Oh, Blaise," she cried, "I'm so glad you're here!"
Without further explanation, she led him into the front
room where Papa and Jaqueline were already seated.
Papa was looking stern and Jaqueline appeared to have
been crying. They brightened when they saw Blaise.

As though by habit, Papa greeted Blaise and asked
how Gilberte was doing.

Blaise replied, "She is doing fine. The baby is due any
day now. She said if it's a boy she will name him Etienne."

Papa's expression remained serious as though he had
not heard Blaise's answer.

Blaise continued, "I got the note from Jaqueline that
you needed me at home. What is wrong?"

At his words, Jaqueline began to cry softly.

Papa spoke. "Jaqueline has informed me that she
wants to enter the convent at Port-Royal."

Blaise sat back in his chair and allowed all the tension of his hasty trip to drain out of him. He would have laughed, but he could tell that this was a tense issue. "Papa, didn't you know that Jaqueline has been attending the sermons at Port-Royal?"

His father shrugged. "I consider attending church there to be the same as attending my church in Normandy."

Blaise continued, "Then I guess you didn't know that the preaching there has made Jaqueline question how she should live as a Christian in the world."

Papa shook his head. He looked as though his heart would break. After a long pause, he began, "Entering the convent means denouncing everything in the world. I already lost your mother, I can't lose Jaquette."

All at once Blaise saw the situation from Papa's perspective. Papa had just retired. Perhaps he had hoped to spend his remaining years surrounded by his family.

Blaise knew how ardently Jaqueline's faith burned. He was at a loss to reconcile the deep feelings that each of them had.

Jaqueline flew to Papa's side and threw her arms around him. "I understand," she cried. "I won't enter the convent during your life, dear Papa."

Papa returned her embrace.

Blaise felt relieved, but he felt sad, too. He knew that one day he would lose his sister to the convent. It made his own goals and ambitions seem more uncertain than ever.

During the next three years Blaise continued to grapple with God's will for his life. He continued to attend the sermons at Port-Royal, and he continued to research and write about the vacuum. Sometimes when he saw Jaqueline at prayer in her room, he felt a pang of guilt that he was not as devoted as she was. At other times, he felt at peace over his decision to continue his work. However, the greatest trial he had yet faced was close at hand.

★ ★ ★ ★ ★ ★ ★ ★ ★ ★ ★

It was October 17, 1651. Blaise carefully smoothed the page of the Bible that lay in his lap. The words he had just translated echoed in his mind. "We are more than conquerors through Him that loved us." It was over three weeks since Papa had died and still every passage Blaise studied reminded him of his father's death. Blaise concentrated on the last verse. Yes, we are more than conquerors through Christ. Even death has no sting.

Swiftly, Blaise reached for the paper, pen, and ink that were always close at hand. He began to write his thoughts with a rapidity that seemed to defy the abilities of the simple quill pen in his hand.

To my dear sister, Gilberte,

In considering Papa's death, we need to look to the person of JESUS CHRIST; for everything in men is abominable. Since God never regards men except through the Mediator JESUS CHRIST, men ought not to regard one another nor themselves, except through the mediation of JESUS CHRIST. For unless we do this, we find in ourselves only true unhappiness, or abominable pleasures. However, if we regard all things through JESUS CHRIST, we shall find full consolation, full satisfaction, full edification."

Blaise leaned back in his chair for a moment to read his words for himself. Suddenly all the Bible texts he had been studying zipped through his mind with one powerful message: JESUS CHRIST. Blaise returned to his writing.

Let us look upon death through JESUS CHRIST, not without JESUS CHRIST. Without JESUS CHRIST it is terrible, detestable, and the ultimate horror in nature. Through JESUS CHRIST it is totally different: it is loveable, holy, and the joy of the believer. All is sweet in JESUS CHRIST, even death.

Blaise allowed the pen to rest in the inkwell. Gilberte would understand his letter. Perhaps it would provide the consolation she needed.

The light from the window dimmed as he wrote. Blaise lit a candle and placed it at his elbow so that he could continue his study of the Bible. He had barely translated a few phrases from the Greek, when there was a gentle knock at his door.

Blaise knew from the sound of the knock that it must be Jaqueline. He rose and opened the door for her. In the darkness of the hallway her face was more pale and thin than ever. Yet this evening the signs of mourning seemed to be lifted. There was a quiet glow in her eyes. Could it be contentment?

Jaqueline did not wait to take a seat. "Blaise, I have come to talk to you about my desire to enter the convent at Port-Royal."

Blaise's peace evaporated. He could only think of how precious his sister was to him. "Jaqueline, must you think about this so soon?"

Jaqueline sensed his thoughts. "You must not think of yourself," she countered. "Even when Papa was alive you agreed with me that this was my calling. I submitted to Papa's wish that I remain with him for his last years. But now I am eager to take my vows. Surely you understand?"

Blaise did understand, but he could not rid himself of the sadness he felt. "Could you give me some time to think?"

"Until Monday." Jaqueline's voice had taken on a quality of strength. She took her brother's hands and gave them a tug as she used to do as a child when trying to get him to play some game. Jaqueline continued, "Then I must obey Christ's calling."

Jaqueline entered the convent the next January. Before she left the world behind, Blaise had one last piece of work to complete. He had to compose the epitaph for Papa. He asked Jaqueline and Gilberte for suggestions. He wanted it to express all that they wanted to say.

For several days he struggled with the wording and content. He sat at his desk, which he had placed next to the window in the hopes of catching the meager sunlight of winter. As he completed the final draft, the mellow January sun broke through the clouds for the first time in days. Blaise lay down his pen and read the epitaph from beginning to end one last time.

Epitaph of M. Pascal, Father

Illustrious for his great knowledge which was recognized by the scholars of all Europe; more illustrious still for the great probity which he exercised in the offices and employments with which he was honored; but much more illustrious for his exemplary piety. He tasted good and bad fortune, that he might be known in every thing for what he was. He was seen temperate in prosperity and patient in adversity. He sought the aid of God in misfortune, and rendered him thanks in happiness. His heart was devoted to his God, his king, his family, and his friends. He had respect for the great and love for the small; it pleased God to crown all the graces of nature that he had bestowed on him with a divine grace which made his great love for God the foundation, the stay, and the consummation of all his other virtues.

Thou, who seest in this epitome the only thing that remains to us of so beautiful a life, admire the fragility of all present things, weep the loss that we have suffered; render thanks to God for having left for a time to earth the enjoyment of such a treasure; and pray his goodness to crown with his eternal glory him whom he crowned here below with more graces and virtues than the limits of an epitaph permit us to relate.

His grief-stricken children have placed this epitaph on this spot, which they have composed from the fulness of their hearts, in order to render homage to the truth and not to appear ingrates in the sight of God.[2]

[2] Eliot, Charles W., Blaise Pascal, ed., vol. 48 of the Harvard Classics (New York: P. F. Collier and Sons Corporation, 1938) p.365.

Chapter 12

Swept Away

It was the spring of 1653. For Blaise, life was totally changed. His close-knit family life unraveled after his father's death. Jaqueline entered the convent and received a new name: Sister Euphemie. Madame Delfaut returned to her home in Coulommiers. Though Blaise maintained the house in Paris, with its staff of 2 servants, he felt as if he no longer had a "home". Gilberte warmly opened her home to Blaise, but he was reluctant to stay too long. Since his house was near Port-Royal of Paris, he often visited his sister. He was encouraged by her gentle and quiet faith, which was his anchor in the swirling currents of the world.

At the moment he felt that he was close to being swept away by those currents. Blaise had accepted an invitation to travel with his friend, the Duke de Roannez.

He found himself in a coach in the company of the Duke, the Chevalier de Méré, and Damien Miton.

Blaise studied his fellow passengers as they joked among themselves. Despite his important title, the Duke was not arrogant. He wore the latest court fashion, but he did not care that his collar was perpetually askew. Blaise and the Duke had lived in the same neighborhood as children, and had met again as adults. Blaise considered the Duke to be a sincere friend.

The Duke seemed to be searching, though in an aimless fashion, for meaning in life. He reminded Blaise of his own carelessness in respect to God in the days before the Deschamps brothers stayed in his home.

The Chevalier de Méré, on the other hand, was intimidating. He was one of those men who knew a little about everything. He knew Greek, Latin, Italian, Spanish, and Arabic. He was an amateur author and mathematician. His profession was the military, which he considered the foremost calling in the world. For de Méré, every issue was an opportunity for a battle of words. He could make a fine argument for any side of any topic he chose to discuss. His flip-flopping from topic to topic and opinion to opinion unnerved Blaise.

Then there was Damien Miton. He was a financier and seemed to embody everything that would be called "worldly". He told coarse jokes, and liked to act superior to everyone else. "After all," he liked to say, "He who has the most money wins in the end." He and de Méré were incurable gamblers. Blaise wondered if this trip was a good idea or not.

His thoughts were interrupted by a hearty slap on the back and the Chevalier de Méré's booming voice saying, "Pascal could figure it out, couldn't you?"

Blaise quickly abandoned his musings. "Figure out what?"

The Chevalier eyed Blaise as though he knew what Blaise had been thinking. "Miton and I were trying to figure out how many times two dice would have to be thrown to make it worthwhile to gamble on two sixes turning up."

Blaise thought a moment. "You would have to take the number of faces on the dice and figure the number of possible combinations." Blaise did a few calculations in his head. "That means it would be worthwhile to gamble if the dice were to be thrown 25 or more times."

De Méré chuckled and nudged Miton. "See there. I told you he could do it."

Miton looked at Blaise with slightly more appreciation. "I guess that's why they call him `Le grand Pascal'. But I wonder if he could calculate our other problem."

De Méré rubbed his hands together. He was enjoying this game of wits. "Pascal, let's say a game had to be stopped before it was finished. How would you divide the stakes fairly so that each received the part that he would probably win."

Blaise's brain began to churn. He grinned and said, "There ought to be a way, but I'll have to work on it."

"Fine," de Méré responded. "While you work on that, we'll discuss the antics of King Louis XIV and Cardinal Mazarin. Then we'll have an update on calculating our wagers."

But the Chevalier de Méré did not receive an update that afternoon, nor the next.

It was not until several months after the question

was first posed that Pascal could give his answer. His
long time friend, Pierre de Fermat, was enlisted to help
with the pursuit. One part of the challenge was figuring
how many different ways the variable, whether dice or
cards, could be combined. In the process of answering
this question, Pascal discovered a fascinating principle
which he called the arithmetical triangle. If numbers are
formed in rows, so that each number is the sum of the
two numbers above it, like this:

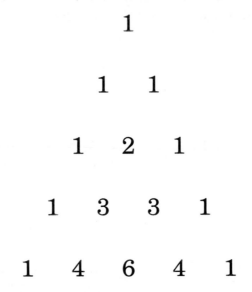

then one can compute the number of possible
combinations of a certain number of objects (for
example, cards) taken a certain number at a time. Thus,
if the game was very simple and there were only four
cards which were to be dealt two at a time, there would
only be three possible combinations. The answer was
determined by going down to the fourth row and (from
left to right) across two. The arithmetical triangle was
used by Pascal and Fermat as a shortcut to determine
several equations that became the foundation of the

branch of mathematics called probability.

Blaise's trip with the Duke de Roannez and the mind-consuming work on probability took their spiritual toll. Late in the summer of 1654, he made a visit to his sister, now known as Sister Euphemie. As he walked through the stone arches of Port-Royal of Paris and past the well-manicured gardens of the courtyard, he longed to have the peace of these outer surroundings inside of him.

He entered the chapel and sat in one of the simple wooden pews. As he had so often done in the past, he studied the vaulted ceiling and beautiful stained glass windows. They usually reminded him of the joy and confidence he had felt as a new Christian, when he first attended sermons here. However, this time the joy and confidence did not come. In agony, he asked himself, "How could I stray so far from God?"

The soft whoosh of a door closing made Blaise aware of his sister's approach. Blaise walked to the wrought iron fence that formed a grille between the nuns and the outside world. Jaqueline was already there. The black wimple of the Port-Royal nuns framed her delicate face. She wore a white robe with a red cross on the front. She smiled warmly at Blaise. "It's so good to see you, Blaise."

Blaise felt at a loss for words.

Jaqueline noticed his uneasiness. "Is there anything wrong?"

Blaise began, "I took a trip with the Duke de Roannez. Do you remember him?"

Jaqueline nodded and waited for Blaise to continue.

"I think I have gradually separated myself from God. I have been busy with other things. It was difficult to attend Church, or even read the Bible during the trip."

Blaise paused, hoping that Jaqueline would interrupt and put in words what he was trying to say, as she so often did. This time she simply listened. Blaise took a deep breath. "Jaqueline, to be honest with you, I have never felt so great an abandonment on God's part as I have felt this year."

Blaise met Jaqueline's eyes and saw that there were tears in them. At that moment the priest entered, and sister and brother had to hurriedly take their seats on their respective sides of the grille. The priest opened the service in Latin, "Derelinquerunt me fontem aquae vivae." Blaise meditated on his words, which were from Jeremiah 2:13. "They have forsaken me the fountain of living waters." He felt as though Jeremiah had been writing about Blaise's own life. He thought of Jesus proclaiming himself to be the living water. Blaise prayed, "Lord, make me to drink of your fountain of living waters."

From that day, Blaise returned to a more serious study of the Bible. As the weeks passed, his faith sent out deeper roots. Fruit began to grow on the branches of his Christian life. Then on the 23rd of November, Blaise recorded a singular experience:

In the year of Grace, 1654,
On Monday, 23rd of November...
From about half past ten in the evening until about half past twelve

FIRE

God of Abraham, God of Isaac, God of Jacob, not of philosophers and scholars.
Certainty. Certainty. Feeling. Joy. Peace.

God of Jesus Christ.
Deum meum et Deum vestrum (My God shall be
your God.)
"Your God shall be my God."
Forgetfulness of the world and of everything,
except God.
He is to be found only by the ways taught
in the Gospel.
Greatness of the human soul.
"Righteous Father, the world has not known thee,
but I have known Thee."
Joy, joy, joy, tears of joy.
I have separated myself from Him.
Derelinquerunt me fontem aquae vivae. (They have
forsaken me the fountain of living waters.)
"My God, wilt thou leave me?"
Let me not be separated from Him eternally.
"This is life eternal, that they might know thee the only
true God, and Jesus Christ, whom thou hast sent."
Jesus Christ.
Jesus Christ.
I have separated myself from Him: I have fled from
Him, denied Him, crucified Him.
Let me never be separated from Him.
We keep hold of Him only by the ways taught
in the Gospel.
Renunciation, total and sweet.
Total submission to Jesus Christ and to my director.
Eternally in joy for a day's exercise on earth.
Non obliviscar sermones tuos. (I will not forget your
words.)
Amen.

Blaise told no one about this experience. He sewed his record of it into the coat he wore. As coats wore out, he transferred it until it was so worn that he had to make a copy. Throughout his life it would be a reminder of the relationship he had with God. The God, who despite Blaise's failings, never would fail him.

Chapter 13

A Wager Between Friends

A few days later Blaise made a visit to the Duke de Roannez. The Duke was in a lively mood. He looked as though he had just awakened. He wore a dressing gown, and his hair was disheveled. On his lap he had some newly-delivered correspondence. "Let me read you this letter that I just received from the Chevalier de Méré. He is so witty!" The Duke began to read, "'It seems to me, that the only logical conclusion one can make in life is that it is pointless to try to learn about God. After all, all the Christian men I know are so dull. Would God really want such narrow people to spend eternity in heaven with him? Life is meant to be a game. I would rather play the game well and leave the men of limited abilities to anguish over the pursuit of God.'"

Pascal held up his hand to interrupt, "My dear

Duke, if I continue to listen to such talk, I will really be made religious."

The smile on the Duke's face faded a little. "What do you mean?"

Pascal sat forward in his chair, hardly able to hide his enthusiasm for the topic. "Atheism shows strength of mind, but only to a certain degree. I approve of men not examining the opinion of Copernicus, but this! It concerns all our life to know whether the soul is mortal or immortal. As for de Méré's contention that it's pointless to try to learn about God, I compare that to an heir who finds the title-deeds of his house and says, `Perhaps they are forged' and does not bother to examine them."

The Duke looked doubtful. "Pascal, I've attended Church all my life, but I've never known if God was there or if the soul is immortal."

Blaise nodded in understanding. "I was the same way, too. I always felt as if I were missing something, as though there were a big vacuum in the middle of my soul. I tried to fill the vacuum with things, success, hobbies, the affection of my friends and family, but nothing satisfied. I came to realize that only God could fill that vacuum. The God who makes Himself known in the Bible."

A hungry look sprang to the Duke's eyes. "Do you mean to say that you can know God?"

Blaise studied his friend for a moment, then asked, "Are you looking for the truth with all your heart?"

The Duke slowly nodded his head.

Blaise continued, "Think about your answer carefully, because once you hear the truth you must deal with it honestly. You must not affirm the truth only so far as it is consistent with your own interests."

When Blaise was satisfied that the Duke was serious, he began his explanation of the Bible. "The Christian religion is very simple. It is based on two facts: first, that there is a God whom men can know, and second, there is a corruption in their nature which makes them unworthy of Him."

The Duke interrupted. "I don't understand. How can we know God if this corruption stands in the way."

Blaise could not help smiling. "That is the most important part of Christianity. It is the only religion that takes care of man's imperfection. The Bible tells us that we have a mediator between God and man: Jesus Christ. You see, God is not simply the author of mathematical truth or the order of the elements, as some would have us think. The God of the Christian is the same one who has been unfolding a plan to save man since the beginning of the world. You can read in the Bible of hundreds of prophecies and miracles that all lead to the coming of Jesus Christ to suffer in our place so that we can know God."

The Duke still had a question. "But what about the people who say that Christianity was invented by the disciples?"

Blaise took his friend's question seriously. In detail he explained how the disciples would have been incapable of manipulating the fulfillment of so many prophecies and of publishing data about the miracles Jesus did if they were not true. The prophecies had been around for hundreds of years and involved things that no one could have controlled such as where Jesus was born, how he would die, etc. The miracles were seen by thousands of eye-witnesses who were still alive when the gospels were written. Jesus' case was made even stronger by the fact that the Jews who did not believe in him were the very ones who preserved the old testament prophecies about him. Blaise concluded, "Our religion is wise and foolish. It is wise because it is the most learned and the most founded on miracles, prophecies, etc. It is foolish, because it is not all this which makes us believe in it. It is the cross that makes us believe."

The Duke was frowning in concentration. "You have given me a lot to think about. Could you come back tomorrow and discuss this further?"

Blaise assured his friend that he would come.

In the days that followed, the Duke became more and more excited about the things he was learning. He found the family Bible, and Blaise conducted him through its pages like a tour guide on a trip through the history of the world. He learned about the myriad of prophecies, miracles and pictures that God used to instruct believers in all ages about the One who would come to deal with man's sin once and for all. One afternoon the two men were sitting in the Duke's study where a hearty fire was roaring in the fireplace. They were enjoying a new drink called hot cocoa. It was becoming popular in Paris, despite some doctors' warnings that it was dangerous to one's health. They sipped their drink in silence. Both seemed lost in their thoughts. Blaise was the first to speak. "You must wager, you know."

The Duke shook himself as though he was just waking up. "What are you talking about?"

Blaise continued. "Faith is like a wager. You can know everything about the Bible, but not have faith. At some point you have to take that step. If you do nothing, you still have made a choice. From the time every person is born, he is embarked on the process that will end in the choice for better or for worse. Which will you choose, then? By wagering for God, at most you risk for a finite time, leading a rather noble life. In order to obey God, you may have to give up things that the world finds harmless, like lying or stealing. You might even have to give up things that the world calls pleasure, but the Bible calls sin. However, by wagering against God, you risk losing an eternity of infinitely happy life. In light of the odds, it would be fair to say that if you gain, you gain everything. If you lose, you lose nothing."

The Duke stared into his cup of cocoa. "I understand what you are saying. I was thinking the same thing." He paused for a moment, then said, "Yes, I'm ready to believe."

That afternoon the Duke accepted the wager and believed. His life was never the same. He was so eager to grow in his faith, that he had a permanent apartment set up in his home so that Blaise could stay for longer visits. He brought everyone he knew to Blaise, as though they were birds with broken wings who needed Blaise's attention. With all of them, Blaise would first ask, "Are you seeking with all your heart?"

The Duke's sister, Charlotte, was one of the first to put her faith in Jesus Christ. When Pascal would return home, he would correspond with the Duke and his sister.

No matter how busy Blaise became with other projects, he took his ministry to his friends seriously. One morning he awoke early to try to finish the letter he was writing to the Duke and his sister. Somehow it was hard to explain all that was in his heart. He was trying to answer a question they had about suffering.

I have learned that in every thing that happens

there is something worthy of admiration, since the will of God is shown in it.

One must not think that the Christian's life is a life of sadness. We forsake pleasures only for other pleasures that are greater. "Pray without ceasing," says St. Paul, "in every thing give thanks, rejoice evermore." It is the joy of having found God that is the reason for the sorrow of having offended him, and for the whole change of life. He that finds a treasure in a field, according to Jesus Christ has such joy that he goes directly and sells all that he has to purchase the field. The people of the world know nothing of this joy, "which the world can neither give nor take away," as is said by Jesus Christ..."In the day of prosperity be joyful; but in the day of adversity consider," says the Scripture. Our joy will not be full until the promise of Jesus Christ is accomplished in us. Therefore, let us not be cast down by sadness, nor believe that piety consists only in bitterness without consolation. The true piety, which is found perfect only in heaven, is so full of satisfaction that it overflows with it...

Chapter 14

Retreat

The wind whipped through Blaise's coat and threatened to extinguish the light he carried. On this January morning of 1655, the chill penetrated to the bone. Several heavily clad figures, each with his own light, joined Pascal as he walked towards the chapel at Port-Royal of the Country. The chapel was in the middle of a cluster of buildings which comprised the community at Port-Royal of the Country. Nestled in the Chevreuse Valley, the convent had become a sheltering place not only for the nuns, but also for many scholars who desired to devote themselves to Bible study and prayer. As Blaise passed through the courtyard, the white stone of the surrounding buildings was barely discernible, and the peaked, red tiled roofs seemed to melt into the darkness of early dawn. Blaise paused a moment to consider the well in the middle of the courtyard. He had an idea that would enable even a twelve-year-old child to raise and lower buckets that contained as much as nine ordinary buckets.

The procession reached the chapel and entered through the simple stone arches. The austere interior of the chapel gave an air of humility to worship. The men began by singing a hymn, unaccompanied by anything save the Port-Royal roosters which had begun to crow. The men's deep voices echoed against the vaulted ceiling. As their hearty praise filled the tiny chapel, Blaise forgot the cold and discomfort. For a moment, heaven did not seem so far away.

The sermon that morning was by Monsieur de Saci and was particularly stirring. After the sermon Monsieur de Saci greeted Blaise warmly. "We're glad that you have joined us," he began. "We could use your help with our translation of the Bible into French."

Blaise felt honored. He had never been among men who knew so much about the Bible. They quoted Scripture constantly. He knew participating in their translation of the Bible would be a challenging experience.

Later during Blaise's retreat he found himself seated at a large table with the scholars who were doing the translating work. Monsieur de Saci opened the meeting and asked another man to read the text that would be discussed. The deep voice of the man as he read from the original Greek text was interrupted only by the crackle of pages being turned as the men compared their own texts and notes to the words. Blaise, too, had come prepared with his own notes. He was eager to discuss a certain passage.

The verses leading up to the passage required several hours of discussion. As the hours passed, several men began to rub their eyes. Feet could be heard shuffling restlessly under the table. As the man with the deep voice read the translated text, now in its tenth revision, it looked as though some participants might fall asleep to the rhythm of his sonorous voice. Blaise glanced at Monsieur de Saci. At least he still sat straight and alert in his chair. Perhaps they would get to that passage today.

When the man finished reading, Monsieur de Saci cleared his throat. A few heads bobbed up at the sound. "It would appear," Monsieur de Saci began, "that we have almost finished our work for today. I would suggest that we adopt for the last sentence the literal translation of the Latin text. Are all in agreement?"

The men had barely begun to rustle through their notes to check the passage before Blaise spoke up. "I disagree." It was the first word he had spoken, and several heads turned in his direction. Blaise elaborated, "The Latin translation does not stress the real meaning behind the Greek words. The Jews were angry with Jesus because he was claiming to be God. I would suggest something like, `Being man, you make yourself God.' People have to come to grips with the fact that Jesus was not just a good man. He claimed to be God and those who heard him understood what he was saying. They had to accept him for all that he was: both man and God, or else grit their teeth and call him a blasphemer, which is what they were doing here."

There was complete silence while Blaise explained his objection. When he finished the men were thoughtful. Several were smiling and nodding their heads in agreement. Monsieur de Saci consulted his Greek text. At last he said, "I would change my proposal to translate the last sentence as Monsieur Pascal so admirably put

it." This time all were in agreement. The men closed the
meeting with a hymn to Jesus, the Son of God.

Blaise emersed himself in the study of the Bible. He
continued to use his knowledge of Greek to more
accurately translate some passages upon which the Latin
version of the Bible was not clear. As he got to know the
other scholars better, he enjoyed spending time with
them outside of the translation sessions. He amazed
them with his ability to tell them the exact place in the
Bible where any verse they quoted could be found.

Blaise also wrote a harmony of the four gospels. It was
the first work of its kind, showing how the events of each
gospel were interwoven. Blaise's goal was to demonstrate
how consistent and trustworthy the Scriptures were.

During his retreat, Blaise was asked to write
textbooks on reading and math for the Port-Royal school.
His own nieces and nephews attended the school, along
with a particularly gifted young man by the name of
Jean Baptiste Racine. He would one day become one of
the greatest writers of French poetic drama. Blaise
enjoyed visiting the students in their classroom. He
found the classroom a fertile place for observations on
human nature. He tried to discover what motivated the
children. He noticed how some children fell into
carelessness, while others pushed themselves to excel.

Near the end of 1655 he wrote "Writings on Grace."
As Blaise went deeper and deeper into his study of the
Bible, the layers of pride were gradually stripped away.
He acknowledged as never before how dependent he was
on God. He wrote, "Salvation springs from the will of
God, and damnation from the will of man." and, "Lord, I
am poor, and a beggar."

Blaise radically changed his goals. He realized that his earlier endeavors in math and physics had been motivated by a desire to forward his own name. He remembered how Jaqueline and he had often talked about the parable of the talents and what it meant. Now he wanted his work to be for God's glory. He decided that he would no longer attach his name to his work. His goal was "Talentum Deo Soli". (My talent for God alone.) One day as he sat staring at these Latin words, he began scrambling them in his mind. Ever since his work on combinations, sequences seemed to form and reform into new combinations in his head. The letters scrambled into three men's names:

Louis de Montalte
Amos Dettonville
Salomon de Tultie

These names became the pen names he used.

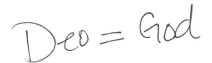

Chapter 15

Attack

It was another January day like the day of Blaise's first retreat at Port-Royal of the Country. Once again Blaise found himself in the small chapel. On this particular day, only a year later, the atmosphere was radically changed. The community at Port-Royal was under attack. Their leader Antoine Arnauld had been condemned by the Sorbonne, the leading theological school of the day. He was criticized for defending the Biblical accuracy of some propositions in Jansen's "Augustinus". Arnauld, himself, spoke at chapel that morning. As he spoke, he gripped the podium. "You who are young should help," he challenged his audience.

To Blaise's surprise, Monsieur Arnauld singled him out after the service. "Blaise, I want you to write in our defense. We can publish pamphlets and perhaps we can reverse the Sorbonne's condemnation."

Blaise replied, "I would like to help, but I really do not understand all the issues myself."

Arnauld nodded. "There are several people, including me, who can give you the information you need. We need someone who is trained in writing persuasively." Arnauld chuckled. "Your debates with Father Noel give you all the qualifications you need."

Blaise was not as confident as Monsieur Arnauld that he had the right qualifications. This sort of defense had to arouse intense popular support so as to change people's opinions.

Back at home, Blaise sat before a blank piece of paper. His pen was at his elbow, but he did not pick it up. Instead he wrestled with the question of how to write such a defense. How could he write without sounding conceited? He knew how difficult it was for him to be humble when he was convinced he was right. But he must lay aside his own convictions if he was to be appealing!

Slowly, he began to build a scene in his mind. He would write as one who was ignorant of the issues. One by one, he would interview experts on each side of the controversy. He would ask the necessary questions to clarify each position and leave the issue unresolved for a while. He smiled as he thought how he could gradually build the suspense, all the while leading his audience on to a better understanding of how correct Monsieur Arnauld's beliefs were.

Only when the outline of his plan was framed in his mind did he begin to write. His thoughts flowed rapidly onto the paper. The fire dwindled to a few red coals before he finished. He signed his name as "Louis de Montalte", and sprinkled the ink with sand to blot it.

There! That would give them something to think about.

For the next few months "Louis de Montalte" kept French society tantalized and the Sorbonne theologians chagrinned with his adept unfolding of the Arnauld controversy. His writings were called "The Provincial Letters" because the author claimed to be a simple, country gentleman from one of the provinces. They were written in logical, clear sentences that were both sensitive and lively. In time, Pascal would become known as the Father of the French prose style for his writing in the "Letters".

Despite the success of "The Provincial Letters", Arnauld was expelled from the Sorbonne. Blaise continued to write letters in defense of Arnauld and Jansenism, because by now the authority of the Bible was at stake. His letters sparkled with wit and insight. He often wrote as though unaware of the evils of those who opposed the Bible. This style made the errors of his opposition even more obvious. The enemies of the Jansenists tried in vain to discover the real author of the letters.

In front of a long row of town houses, a man in the black robe of the clergy paused for a moment to consult a piece of paper tucked in his sleeve. In the dim light of dusk he appeared to have a difficult time deciding which door to try. He chose a door in the middle of the row and knocked softly. Immediately the door opened and the man slipped inside. One by one, other men dressed in similar garb, cautiously approached the door and disappeared through the doorway.

Inside the house, both the shutters and curtains were closed tightly. The only light came from a single candle, deep in the interior of the house. It was placed on a table where eight men were talking in low voices. Blaise sat between two of the men. He was writing as fast as they could talk. From time to time, one of the men would leave the room and check that the door and windows were still secure. No one could know that this meeting was taking place, or who was attending it. Despite the serious faces of the other men, Blaise was enjoying the secretive atmosphere of the meeting. What would the theologians at the Sorbonne think if they knew that the collaborators and author of "The Provincial Letters" were meeting only a few blocks from them?

There was a pause in the discussion, and Blaise took the opportunity to clarify the information he had received. "Are you saying that there are theologians who think a person is not a sinner if he never thinks about God?"

The men nodded.

A slow smile began to spread across Blaise's face. "Gentlemen, I think I have the information I need. Thank you for your time."

Just then, one of the men rushed in hissing in an urgent whisper, "Stop now! Everyone must leave! Quickly! Quickly!"

Silently the men filed out the back door. Blaise watched as their black robes melted into the darkness. He turned and swaggered on his cane as he made his way home.

The next week, the fourth "Provincial Letter" was published. The "naive" country gentleman exposed the careless morals of the Jansenist's adversaries with such insight and humor that he won many more supporters. He wrote:

> *"Oh, my dear sir," I cried, "what good news this will be to some people I know! I really must introduce them to you. You have probably never in your whole life, met people who had fewer sins by the way you account for it....I always thought that the less a man thought about God, the more he was sinning, but, I see now that if one never thinks about God, he will be considered pure forever. Away with your half-way sinners, who still have a sneaking affection for doing right. They will all be condemned, these semi-sinners."*

By the time the last letter was published on March 24, 1657, popular sympathy for the Jansenists had been won. For a while it seemed that the Sorbonne would relax the persecution of the Jansenists. Meanwhile, Blaise saw a need for a broader defense of the Christian faith. He began to tap the mental notes he had stored all his life. As the thoughts surfaced, he wrote them on the first scrap of paper that came to hand. Blaise had a growing compassion for those, like the Duke's friends, who did not yet know God's grace. On one piece of paper he scribbled:

> *Imagine a number of men in chains and all condemned to die. Each day, some are killed in the view of the others, and those who remain see their own fate in that of their fellows. Looking at each other sorrowfully and without hope, they wait their turn. It is the image of the condition of men."*

On another scrap of paper he wrote:

A man in a dungeon with only one hour to appeal his case, would act unnaturally in spending that hour playing piquet.

Then he wrote:

This religion requires us to always regard others as capable of the grace which can enlighten them. We must call upon them to have pity upon themselves and take at least some steps in the endeavor to find light.

Blaise's convictions increasingly spread to every area of his life. In an effort to make the best use of his resources for God, he moved to a less expensive home. He dismissed his servants, which meant that he had to do his own housework and make his own meals. In his usual methodical fashion, he determined the amount of food that would be necessary for him and never exceeded that amount. When Gilberte visited once, she was surprised by the simplicity of his food. "Let me make you some sauces and relishes," she said. But Blaise insisted that he was content with his simple food.

Blaise also sold his coach, horses, fine furniture, silverware, and his library except for his Bible, a few devotionals, and the works of Saint Augustine. He managed the small fortune that his father had left him so that he could devote as much as possible to God's work.

Despite his poor health, he rallied every ounce of energy to write his defense of Christianity. From time to time he would touch the place in his coat where he had sewn the record of that special night. It would renew his desire to live for God.

Chapter 16

Thwarted

Blaise clutched his right cheek where the toothache sent wrenching pains into his head. The damp, cold air of his room seemed to make the pain worse, but Blaise was reluctant to indulge himself in a larger fire in the fireplace. He tried biting down on a whole clove as Madame Delfaut had suggested in her last letter. Still, he could not rid himself of the pain.

The clatter of hooves on the street below signalled the arrival of the Duke de Roannez's coach. Blaise wrapped his coat tightly around himself and prepared to join the Duke. At the last moment he snatched up a loose pile of papers. "Perhaps these will keep my mind off my toothache," he told himself.

The Duke was delighted to see his friend. He was just beginning a lighthearted update of how his family was faring, when he noticed Blaise's swollen cheek. "Blaise, what is wrong with your cheek?"

Blaise slumped deeper into the seat of the coach. "It's only a toothache, but the pain is intense."

The Duke was concerned. "Do you have anything to help the pain?" He knew Pascal was becoming too thrifty to buy the medicines he needed.

Blaise held up the pile of papers. "Only these. Nothing else helps."

The Duke looked skeptically at the papers, which did not remotely resemble a proper remedy. "What are these? Your current project?"

Blaise smiled wryly. "I thought I was done with mathematics, but it seems to be the only thing that can distract me from this toothache." The wheel of the coach hit a rut in the road, and Blaise winced in pain.

The Duke noticed his friend's expression and tried to aid in the distraction. "Could you explain it to me?"

Blaise straightened in the seat and considered his explanation for a moment. "It concerns the cycloid. A cycloid is the curve made by a point on a circle as the circle turns along a straight line."

The Duke gave him a puzzled look. Blaise tried again. Pointing through the window, he said, "Do you see that coach next to us? Imagine that there is an ant on the rim of one of the wheels. Can you see what his path would be like as the coach rolls down the road?"

The Duke watched intently as the wheels of the coach turned. Suddenly he let out a cry of triumph. "I see it! It looks like this." He traced a few humps in the air.

Blaise felt triumphant, too. "That's right." He flipped through the papers and held up the last page for the Duke to see. "I think that I have here the solution to the

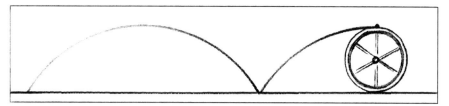

A cycloid is the curve made by a point on a circle as the circle turns along a straight line.

cycloid."

"That is wonderful!" The Duke responded enthusiastically. He paused for a moment, then asked. "How is your Defense of the Christian Religion coming?"

"Fine," Blaise replied. "Why do you ask?"

"I was just thinking," the Duke paused. He seemed reluctant to continue. He tried again, "I was just thinking that you will be publishing it under a pen name, and your pen name will need to establish a name for himself. Why don't you pose a contest for the problem of the cycloid and have your pen name solve the problem? That would establish his credibility to write the defense of Christianity."

Blaise marvelled at his friend's ingenuity. It reminded him of the Bible passage that said, "Be ye therefore wise as serpents and harmless as doves." That afternoon the "Contest for the problem of the Cycloid" began.

Blaise worked hard to prepare his theorems for public competition. Noted mathematicians of the day, including Wallis and Lalouère accepted the challenge. Though only Pascal's "Amos Dettonville" was able to provide the complete solution, the two contest-makers had not anticipated how tricky it would be to establish that Amos Dettonville had figured the solution independently of the other contestants. Instead of bringing credibility and fame, the contest brought suspicion and discontent. Blaise felt thwarted. He wondered if he would be able to communicate the precious truths of the Bible without being misunderstood. Nevertheless, he continued to write his thoughts on scraps of paper. The pieces of ideas were growing into piles which Blaise sorted and tied together in a rough order.

In his despair over the contest, Blaise resorted to the Bible for comfort. He composed an essay which he titled the Mystery of Jesus. In the essay he wrote, "Lord, I give thee all."

In the face of Jesus Christ's overwhelming gift of grace, Blaise knew that he must give ALL: his work, his hopes for the contest, his pride, even his desire for good health.

"Lord, I give thee all."

Chapter 17

The Plan of Defense

Once again Blaise was visiting the chapel at Port Royal. This time, however, he was standing at the front instead of sitting in one of the pews. The scholars at Port-Royal had asked him to present the plan for his Defense of the Christian Religion which he hoped to write. Blaise knew that his health was failing. He realized that he could probably sustain only one year of intellectual work, though the defense he was writing would require ten years of good health. Despite these limitations, he agreed to address the group at Port-Royal.

Blaise took a moment to look around the room. He recognized many faces from the days when they had met secretly to write "The Provincial Letters". Behind the seated men, the white stone of the chapel seemed to have a light of its own. The stained glass windows glowed like jewels in their setting of roughly-hewn rock. Blaise returned his gaze to the podium before him. It was worn smooth where generations of faithful men had gripped it as they spoke. Blaise gingerly placed his sheaf of notes on its broad surface and waited for the meeting to begin.

At last Monsieur Singlin opened the meeting. He laughed as he said that Monsieur Pascal needed no introduction. Blaise nervously found his place in his notes and began:

> *Men scorn the Christian religion. They hate it and fear that it is true. To remedy this, we must begin by showing that Christianity is not at all contrary to reason. We must show that it is venerable, so as to inspire respect for it. We must show that it is loveable, so as to make good men hope it is true. Finally, we must prove it is true."*

Blaise looked up from his notes and realized that everyone was listening intently. He relaxed his grip on his notes and continued:

> *I know what some of you are thinking. I want to make it clear that I am not saying that this Defense of the Christian Religion will cause people to become Christians. I believe that the plan of God, who disposes all things kindly, is to put religion into the mind by reason, and into the heart by grace.*

Blaise paused for a moment to see if there were any objections to his statement. Unlike the time when he talked with Monsieur de Rebours, his audience seemed to understand the place that Pascal gave to reason. He met the eyes of those in the audience and his voice took on a new note of earnestness as he spoke:

*We must persuade men to seek the truth without
hesitation. We must warn them that if they refuse it,
they show that they value the esteem of men more than
the search for truth. For the Christian religion has as
much evidence and as many signs of certainty as the
things which are the least doubted in this world.*

From that point Blaise outlined for them the content
of his defense. First he would sketch a picture of man
with which a broad-minded intellectual could identify.
Next he would draw from philosophers and religions of
the world to demonstrate man's limitations and need for
God. Then he would present the Jewish people and
explain how God blessed them in preparation for Jesus
Christ. This would naturally lead to a deeper look at the
Old Testament with its explanation of the Fall of man,
climaxing in a clear exposition of God's plan of
redemption in both the New and Old Testaments. In this
way, he hoped to bring an intellectual to understand that
beyond the truth of what we can see and feel, there is the
truth which God has revealed in the Bible.

Blaise's presentation was received well. His
colleagues encouraged him to continue his work. Etienne
Périer, Blaise's nephew, was in the audience. Pascal
noted with approval that he and many other young men
were taking notes. Blaise thought, "If I do not finish the
work, perhaps they will carry it to completion."

Back at home, Blaise collapsed on his bed. The exertion
of the travelling and the presentation had exhausted him.
He pulled his Bible to him and began to read. One phrase
caught his attention. It was Paul writing to the church at

Philippi, telling them of the privilege of sharing in Christ's sufferings. As Blaise read the verses again, joy swelled in his heart that he could share in Christ's sufferings. He grabbed his pen and scrawled a prayer:

> *Grant me the favor, Lord, to join thy consolations to my sufferings, that I may suffer like a Christian....I ask not to have the fullness of consolation without any suffering; for this is the life of heaven. Neither do I ask to be in the fullness of evils without consolation; for this is the state of the Jews. But I ask, Lord, to feel at the same time both sorrow for my sins, and the consolations of thy Spirit through thy grace; for this is the true condition of Christianity.*

> *I ask of thee neither health, nor sickness, nor life, nor death; but that thou wilt use my health and my sickness, my life and my death, for thy glory, for my salvation, and for the utility of the Church and of thy saints, of whom I hope by thy grace to form a part. Thou alone knowest what is best for me. Thou art the sovereign master. Do what thou wilt. Give to me, take from me; but conform my will to thine. Grant that in holy confidence and in humble and perfect submission, I may welcome the plan thou hast for my life, and that I may adore alike all that comes to me from thee.*

Blaise read over the prayer he had written. When he came to the words "Church" and "saints", he paused for a moment.

It seemed that their meanings had become distorted in these times. People thought of the Church as consisting of all those who went to church services. The Bible, however, clearly stated that the true Church was made up of those whose hearts were right with God. That was not true of everyone who attended church. It was not even true of all those who held powerful positions in the church. There were so many things that were done in the name of the "Church" that were not in agreement with what God said in the Bible. As for the word, "saint", people like Friar Forton were teaching that it was a term only for the super-Christians. The Bible, however, clearly taught that all who are saved through Jesus Christ are called "saints". Blaise decided to leave the words as they were written. He knew that God understood.

Chapter 18

Standing Firm

Soon after Blaise's presentation to the scholars at Port Royal, the Jansenists began to experience persecution. The school at Port-Royal received the order that no new students would be allowed to enroll. A few months later the school was dispersed altogether. The boarders and novices of the two convents were expelled, and no new novices were accepted. The leaders of Port-Royal had to go into hiding. Only the nuns of Port-Royal remained, and they were now being forced to sign a statement that read, "I condemn with heart and mouth the doctrine of the five Propositions of Cornelius Jansen contained in his book entitled, `Augustinus'."

Many of the nuns signed the statement by adding their reservations to it before their signature. However, the political forces in the Church were on a mission to crush the Jansenist movement, and they ruthlessly refused to accept the signatures with the reservations. Jaqueline, now Sister Euphemie, held out as long as she could. She stuck to her convictions of the truth of the Bible, and said, "Since the bishops have the courage of maids, the maids should have the courage of bishops."

A meeting was called at Blaise's home to determine what should be done. Blaise paced nervously back and forth in the sparsely furnished room that served as his study. Gilberte was staying with him because of his poor health. She scolded Blaise. "You need to relax. This meeting will be taxing enough on your strength. Please, sit down."

Blaise stopped and rested on his cane. "I cannot believe that Arnauld was counseling the nuns to sign the statement. It is wrong!"

Gilberte interjected, "But you know that he feels responsible for them. He can't ask them to risk their lives for a question of conscience."

Blaise stiffened. "There is more than this life to consider..."

He was interrupted by a knock on the door. Blaise's nephew, Etienne, burst in before Gilberte had time to open the door. His face was white, and he had not taken off his riding coat which was splattered with mud. "I just came from Port-Royal. Sister Euphemie died this morning. The doctor said it was tuberculosis."

Gilberte began to cry softly. Blaise sat down. He thought of his sister as a child, playing "Hotel des Vernines"...Jaquette, standing on a chair to dramatize her complaints about studying grammar...as a young actress and poet, deepened by her brush with smallpox... finally as an ardent Christian who would not compromise the truth. Blaise met Gilberte's eyes and said, "May we all die as well as that."

Soon after, the people began arriving for the meeting. There were Monsieur Arnauld, the Duke de Roannez, and many leaders of Port-Royal. Etienne was to stay to take notes.

As the meeting progressed it became clear that the majority favored a compromise to allow the nuns to sign the statement. As Arnauld said, "We need to maintain the unity of the Church. If the Pope has ordered this statement to be signed then we must submit in silence, without these `reservations'."

Blaise immediately rose to his feet. "Silence is the greatest persecution. The saints have never been silent. It is true that we are being called to act, but not by the Pope who is requiring this odious signature. We are being called by necessity to defend the truth. The more unjustly we are censured and the more violently our speech is stifled, the more loudly we must cry out. One day a righteous Pope will come who will side with justice. Until then, we must cry out." The Duke and Etienne Périer agreed with Pascal.

Arnauld, however, shook his head. "No, we have already consulted among ourselves, and we can't afford to oppose the signature. It could split the Church." He sat down as though there was nothing left to discuss.

Blaise could not believe what he was hearing. "I disagree," he said heatedly, "There is no difference between condemning the doctrine of Jansen on the five propositions and condemning the Bible."

At that comment Arnauld jumped to his feet. His eyes were flashing in indignation and he gripped the table as he did when agitated. "Monsieur Pascal does not

seem to realize that "The Provincial Letters" have been
condemned by the Inquisition and thus, the Pope. It
would be unwise to continue in that course."

Blaise looked around the table at each man in turn. He
tried to keep his voice calm. "Are you willing to
compromise the truth? Don't you think that the
compromise of the truth is just as bad as the
manufacturing of falsehood? The Inquisition and the entire
society that controls it are the two scourges of the truth. If
you give in, you will be just as guilty as they are of
misleading the people."

Besides the Duke and Etienne, Blaise met with blank
stares. These were the same men who had secretly met
with him to supply him with the information to write
"The Provincial Letters". They had fought together for
the truth. Even when under attack, there had been a
security in knowing that one was not fighting alone. But
now the very people who had always been the defenders
of the truth were wavering. Blaise thought of Papa's
words from so many years ago. "God is always the same.
It is men who change."

Blaise could feel the pressure mounting in his head.
His face felt hot and suddenly the room seemed painfully
bright. He turned to Monsieur Arnauld and said, "You
say that my "Letters" are condemned in Rome. That
would make me a heretic. Do you believe that I am truly
a heretic? If you are afraid of the Pope's judgement,
shouldn't you be even more afraid of God's judgement?"
Blaise clutched his cane and turned stiffly to each person
in turn. "If my "Letters" are condemned at Rome, I
condemn in Rome that which is condemned in heaven."
The room began to sway. Silently Blaise cried out to God,
"To thy tribunal, Lord Jesus, I appeal."

When Blaise returned to consciousness, Gilberte was hovering over him with a look of concern. "Blaise, what happened?"

Blaise was grim. "I am learning what it means to obey God rather than men. But I possess the truth, and no one can take that away."

Gilberte could not hide her fears about Blaise's health. "Blaise, I think you should come back to Clermont with me. I can take care of you better there."

"But there is still much I must do here." Blaise remonstrated.

"Bring your work with you, only let me help you with the writing. You will wear yourself out if you keep pushing yourself." Gilbert replied.

Blaise was firm. "I must stand up for the truth, even if I must stand alone."

Blaise did not go to Clermont at that time. He remained in Paris and used every ounce of his failing energy to work on his *Defense of the Christian Religion*. Now, more than ever, he saw the need for it.

The Wager Fulfilled

It was a day that would go down in history books. On this day in 1662, the first omnibus clattered its way around Paris. Seven carriages driven by coachmen in bright blue smocks, bearing the royal insignia, picked up passengers at Luxembourg every half hour and transported them along a designated route to Porte St. Antoine. It was the first public mass-transportation system in the world.

Blaise Pascal developed the idea of the omnibus as a way to help poor people who did not have access to coaches. As usual, the Duke de Roannez backed his friend's invention, and the omnibus became a reality. They formed a stock company complete with a royal license. They announced that the omnibus was "open to all and for all." It was an overnight success, and soon people found that they could not even get a seat because the carriages were full.

Meanwhile, Blaise became more and more concerned with how he could help the poor. He sold his share in the omnibus venture so that he could help relieve the victims of a famine in a nearby province. When he no longer had any possessions to sell, he opened his home to a homeless family. A few weeks later, the son contracted smallpox. Blaise did not want to turn them out, so he took Gilberte's invitation to come to Clermont.

Blaise enjoyed the coach ride to Clermont. He watched the rolling countryside just outside of Paris give way to the mountains and valleys of Auvergne, the province where he was born. As the Puy de Dome came into view, Blaise welcomed it like an old friend. Like truth, it never changed. He remembered a small black stone and a young boy asking questions about what was real. Now Blaise realized that there are some things that are more real than what can be seen and felt.

At last the coach rolled through the gates of Clermont. The vegetable gardens that surrounded the wall were almost ready for harvest. Inside the gates, children in ragged clothing stopped their games to stare at the coach. Their mothers peered from the yawning doorways of homes whose crumbling walls seemed to be little more than a heap of rocks. Blaise wondered how he could soften their suffering. The coach picked its way up the narrow winding streets to the market section. Here, rows of shops leaned into the street. On this fine summer day, their shutters were wide open. Blaise glimpsed the faces of successful, satisfied merchants smoking their pipes. They were quite a contrast to the ragged children, but Blaise knew they had needs as well. His attention was caught by the sturdy, square outline of the cathedral, rising above the jumble of buildings. It crowned the brow of the hill, for all to see: the poor and the rich, the believers and the seekers. Just then, the coach lurched to a stop in front of a plain stone house. The only indication that it was the home of a distinguished councilor was a small emblem above the door. Gilberte opened the door before the coach even stopped, and welcomed her brother warmly.

During the next two months Blaise did what he could to get his Defense of the Christian Religion in order. Gilberte took his dictation. Despite all his labor, the project was still a collection of scraps of paper tied in bundles as though in an outline.

Blaise's condition steadily grew worse. The doctors diagnosed tuberculosis. When Gilberte anxiously asked them what they could do, they spread their hands in defeat. "You must do what you can to make your brother comfortable. And keep the priest nearby."

Near the end, Blaise began to suffer from convulsions. During the early hours of August 19th the convulsions followed one after another. Blaise called for the priest, who administered communion to him. Shortly afterwards, he died.

The funeral was held at the Church of Saint Etienne-du-Mont. On that August morning the light from the stained glass windows cast red and blue colors on the stone arches of the church. The small church could barely hold all who came to pay their last respects. Gilberte and Florin Périer and their children were there. Their son, Etienne Périer, would go on to prepare his uncle's Defense of the Christian Religion for publication. There were Blaise's colleagues from the "Académie

Libre", including Pierre de Fermat who had developed the science of probability with him. The Duke de Roannez and his sister, Charlotte, were there. Charlotte was now a nun at Port-Royal. Arnauld and other Port-Royalists in hiding mingled with the poor who thronged the aisles. All could testify to the sincerity of Blaise Pascal's life.

Blaise once wrote, "Let us act as though we had only eight hours to live." He spent his life trying to live in light of the truth that he had found in God. He stood firm until the end. Now, the wager was fulfilled.

Blaise Pascal's "Defense of Christianity" was left as an unfinished bundle of notes.

Epilogue

Though Blaise Pascal increasingly tried to avoid notoriety, his name is almost a household word today. The programming language, "Pascal", was named in his honor because he designed the first mechanical calculating machine, a forerunner of the modern digital computer. Until World War II, all bus tickets sold in Paris had a picture of Pascal on them, a tribute to the inventor of that system. His name is also attached to advances in many different fields. He is considered the Father of the French prose style. His work on conic sections yielded "Pascal's Theorem" and laid the groundwork for Analytic Geometry. In the field of probability, which he discovered, there is "Pascal's Triangle". (He called it the arithmetical triangle.) His work in probability is also considered the forerunner of Integral Calculus and Newton's Binomial Theorem. Today, probability is used in genetics, life insurance, and many other areas. Pascal's work on the vacuum not only gave birth to the science of Hydrostatics and many useful inventions, but also gave us "Pascal's Law". When you see a calculator, an elevator, or even a bus, remember Pascal.

Despite all these achievements, Blaise Pascal's most enduring contribution to the world is considered to be his Pensées, the thoughts he wrote for the *Defense of the Christian Religion*. They were published just as he left them. For over 300 years, the Pensées have drawn people to consider the truth of God. They are the testimony of a brilliant mind which found ultimate truth in God alone.

Bibliography

Bishop, Morris, **Pascal, The Life of Genius** (Connecticut: Greenwood Press, 1964)

Cailliet, Emile, **Pascal: The Emergence of Genius** (New York: Harper and Brothers, 1961)

Carr, John Lawrence, **Life in France under Louis XIV** (New York: G. P. Putnam's Sons, 1966)

Davidson, Hugh M., ed., **Blaise Pascal** (Boston: Twayne Publishers, 1983)

Duclaux, Mary, **Portrait of Pascal** (New York: Harper and Brothers Publishers, 1927)

Durant, Will and Ariel, **The Age of Louis XIV** (New York: Simon and Schuster, 1963)

Great Books of the Western World, Hutchins, Robert M.,ed., *Pensées* by Blaise Pascal, vol. 33: (Chicago: Encyclopædia Britannica, Inc., 1952)

The Harvard Classics, Eliot, Charles W.,ed., *Blaise Pascal*, vol. 48 (New York: P. F. Collier and Sons Corporation, 1938)

Hazelton, Roger, Blaise Pascal: The Genius of His Thought (Philadelphia: Westminster Press, 1974)

Krailsheimer, A. J., **Pascal** (New York: Hill and Wang, 1980)

Mesnard, Jean, **Pascal**, Claude and Marcia Abraham, translators (Alabama: University of Alabama Press, 1969)

Mortimer, Ernest, **Blaise Pascal: The Life and Work of a Realist** (New York: Harper and Brothers Publishers, 1959)

Nelson, Robert J., **Pascal: Adversary and Advocate** (Massachusetts: Harvard University Press, 1981)

Acknowledgements

All Scriptures are from the King James Version of the Bible.

Quotes written by Pascal (and many quotes used in conversations) are original translations by the author from his works edited by L. Lafuma:

Lafuma, L., **Oeuvres Complètes** L. Lafuma, ed., (Paris: L'Intégrale, 1963)

CPSIA information can be obtained at www.ICGtesting.com
Printed in the USA
LVOW10s1333060916

503427LV00034B/586/P